The Chicago Diaries of

JOHN M. WING

1865–1866

John M. Wing in 1868

The Chicago Diaries of JOHN M. WING 1865–1866

Edited by Robert Williams

Foreword by Paul F. Gehl

Essay by Richard A. Schwarzlose

SOUTHERN ILLINOIS UNIVERSITY PRESS
Carbondale and Edwardsville

THE CAXTON CLUB OF CHICAGO

The diaries presented in this book and all illustrations, except those on pages lxiv and 35, were provided through the courtesy of the Newberry Library, Chicago.

Printed in the United States of America
05 04 03 02 4 3 2 1

Publication partially funded by a subvention grant from The Caxton Club of Chicago.

Library of Congress Cataloging-in-Publication Data

Wing, John M. (John Mansir), 1845–1917.
The Chicago diaries of John M. Wing, 1865–1866 / edited by Robert Williams ; with a foreword by Paul F. Gehl ; with an essay by Richard A. Schwarzlose.
p. cm.
Includes bibliographical references (p.) and index.
1. Wing, John M. (John Mansir), 1845–1917—diaries. 2. Book collectors—Illinois—Chicago—Diaries. 3. Publishers and publishing—Illinois—Chicago—Diaries. 4. Journalists—Illinois—Chicago—Diaries. 5. American newspapers—History—19th century. 6. Chicago (Ill.)—Intellectual life—19th century. I. Williams, Robert, 1936– II. Title.

Z989.W73 A3 2002
070'.5'0977311—dc21

2002018780

ISBN 0-8093-2483-0 (cloth : alk. paper)

The paper used in this publication meets the minimum requirements of American National Standard for Information Sciences—Permanence of Paper for Printed Library Materials, ANSI Z39.48-1992. ∞

Contents

Illustrations

Foreword

The Making of a Chicago Eccentric

SOME YEARS AGO, in an address to the Caxton Club, the late Robert Rosenthal, head of special collections at the University of Chicago libraries, proposed a typology of Chicago book collectors based on his extensive researches into their surviving papers and books. The last of his categories, admittedly a catchall, was composed of "eccentrics," often autodidacts, who collect with passion but not system, following the whims of a lively but disordered intellectual life. One of Rosenthal's prime examples of the type was John Mansir Wing, the subject as well as the author of the youthful, "veracious memoir" featured in this volume. Here Caxtonian Robert Williams, calligrapher and designer at the University of Chicago Press, presents the portion of Wing's diaries that relate his arrival in Chicago, the metropolis of the West, to seek his fortune as a journalist just at the end of the Civil War. They constitute an eccentric self-portrait of a brilliant but callow young man—ambitious, romantic, and vain—and of a glittering, boisterous boomtown filled with new immigrants (from the East, like Wing, and from abroad), new millionaires, and newly demobilized soldiers.

These extracts derive from the last two of nine surviving diaries that tell Jack Wing's story from 1858 to 1866. They carry him from recently graduated, fourteen-year-old schoolboy through several years' apprenticeship first as a typesetter and then as a cub reporter in upstate New York, and then on to the West. In Cleveland, Detroit, Chicago, Waukegan, St. Louis, and New Orleans, Wing tried his hand at journalism, advertising, and small-time publishing. When the diaries break off, he had returned to Chicago again, but at twenty-two years of age he was still not a settled figure. The next few years see him back in New York state, in Boston, and in Europe, making his living mostly as a roving reporter, ever sharp to sell a colorful and entertaining story to the insatiable American press.

Wing would return to Chicago definitively in 1869, where he founded a trade magazine, *The Land Owner,* two years before the Great Fire created opportunities for fortune seeking even greater than those of the Chicago of the 1860s. *The Land Owner* would witness, in type and in lithographed and engraved images, first the boom years before the fire and then the rebirth of the city after it. When the ever restless Wing tired of that subject, he folded the magazine to found a new journal with another popular cause. *The Western Brewer* was also a trade rag, sold to brewers in every town and village of the West. It reported in timely fashion on the Chicago commodities markets and on a wide variety of other news, national and international, of interest to brewers. Moreover, just as *The Land Owner* had risen on the bubble of real-estate speculation, this new journal rode the tides of early prohibitionism with an opportunistic editorial stance. Beer, Wing told his readers, was a wholesome and nutritious Central European food, unlike unhealthful American whisky, which was both an evil recreation in itself and likely to draw the fire of strident and unreasoning prohibitionists—who might just take away our beer as well! However we may judge the sincerity of this pitch, it was both accurate in foresight and well aimed at an interested public. *The Western Brewer* flourished.

Successful in publishing, then, and at speculating in railroad and other shares, John M. Wing retired in 1888 at the age of forty-four. The remainder of his life was devoted to his often eccentric, always obsessive hobbies: international travel, family-history research, book and print collecting, and extra-illustration (augmenting published volumes with prints). For his later life, we know most about the extra-illustrating, because some twenty-two sets (eighty-five volumes in all) survive, always with self-mocking title pages of Wing's own devising and usually his own captions. There are also several scrapbooks from this period. These many albums reveal a scavenger of a collector, disdainful of politicians and of organized religion and impatient with social niceties (he never joined any of the flourishing literary or bibliophile clubs of gilded-age Chicago) but sentimental about family and voracious in his reading of the popular press. All these later interests of Wing, as well as his essential restlessness, are also present in kernel in the diaries of his Chicago adventures.

These diaries have real strengths and definite weaknesses as an historical source. Jack Wing, as he styled himself after his arrival in Chicago, was a complex young man who tells us much about growing up on one's own in midcentury America and about the details of life in booming postwar Chicago. He is amazingly frank in the diaries, so there is little factual to distrust. Moreover, the text is engaging; Wing writes easily and comfortably. He shows no hesitation to use slang when that is the term he knows or to insert a foreign word he has heard but not always understood. There is a callow and sentimental sincerity on every page. But the Jack Wing of the diaries is also very young, and so he is judgmental without being very perceptive.

Wing tells of adventures successful and not, honest and not, savory and not. At twenty-one, of course, he does not much discern. His emotions and opinions are vividly present to himself and to the diary; we can usually trust them. But his ability to judge others is poor, and his will to imagine their motives is almost nil. People are always either helpful and well met or else they are hugely malicious and out to get Jack Wing. Considering that he worked for some of the most influential journalists of the day; interviewed and shared smokes with politicians, businessmen, and war heroes like Sherman and Grant; and met many in the city's demimonde, we learn remarkably little about these famous and infamous figures. Perhaps most of what Wing had to say went into his sensational newspaper pieces, and the diary is left with only lists of names and dates. His perceptions, however, were always limited, a trait particularly evident in his account of his superiors at the newspapers he worked for, men he depended on for a livelihood and whom he did not describe anywhere in print but who acted, to listen to Wing, in totally arbitrary fashion. These are truly his perceptions, but they are not accurate ones; Wing was just too much the egotist to see his colleagues clearly.

Wing's personal relationships are equally ill described. We know of enthusiasms for many individuals; and we find named every old fraternity brother he runs into and every one of the boys of various classes and types that he brings home to bed. But we rarely get much physical description of these individuals, even those newly met, to say nothing of information about their personalities or motives. He is also very reticent (predictably in the 1860s) to describe any physical act of intimacy, even a handshake or pat on the back. And he can also be just plain dim, totally uncomprehending of friends' deeds, as when one steals from him or another wanders off in the middle of the night.

As extraordinary as Wing's professional adventures are, then, his private life seems to have been fairly commonplace, even in his own mind. Like every twenty-year-old, he is hungry for sex, and like most of that age in his America, he takes for granted that boys will often share beds in pairs or in groups and sometimes share sexual intimacies, too. In particular, it was common for slightly older boys to entertain and educate younger ones sexually. In his earliest diaries, Wing is the younger partner; by the time he gets to Chicago, he is usually the elder. But Wing also shared the notion of the day that boys eventually outgrow this youthful promiscuity and, as mature men, marry nice, steady, homemaking women. Jack Wing still fervently believes in and hopes for this outcome in these diaries. Nonetheless, we know that he never married.

Jack Wing's book collecting is another matter, not commonplace at all. He presents it to himself in the diaries as one of his defining characteristics, and it was, in fact, unusual in an American so young. It was also one of his vanities, for he is careful to show to new acquaintances his growing collection of books—he bought some sixty volumes and a suitable bookcase within months of arriving penniless in Chicago. At times, Wing's book collecting seems to be of a piece with his purchases of posh clothes and jewelry, all for the sake of "a delightful rig," as he calls it. But it is interesting that in time of need, he will pawn his watch chain or diamond stickpin, not his books.

Wing's books were passionately acquired but not, it seems, carefully chosen. His reading was totally unsystematic and intuitive, like his newspaper life. He bought books in French that he could not read, for example, but that he thought were old and valuable. Throughout his life, he was enthusiastic about illustrated books, especially biography, history, and travel, and he doted on sentimental English poetry. These volumes, usually contemporary editions, fed his youthful imagination as they would later console his sedentary middle age.

It is disappointing that later diaries do not survive, though of course we cannot expect that if they did they would be quite so lively and naively informative as these. Already in 1866, Wing's resolve to keep up with them is waning. The reason we do have these and do not have later ones, however, is almost surely to be sought in the peripatetic nature of his early life. When he left Chicago to go back East, probably in 1867, Wing apparently did not intend to come back, and so he shipped his beloved books to be stored at the family home. When he returned to the West in 1869, some of these books must have stayed behind, saved from destruction in the fire along with almost everything else John M. Wing owned in Chicago in 1871. Only later did these few volumes come back to the Old Corner Library, as he styled the mature book collection of his retirement. They now reside at the Newberry Library, as do most of Wing's extra-illustrated volumes and the other books he left behind at the time of his death in 1917. The collection and the eccentric collector await further research.

Paul F. Gehl
The Newberry Library

Newspapers in Jack Wing's World

AFTER CENTURIES of haphazard news gathering and painfuly slow hand printing, technology smiled on newspapers in the 1840s, bringing more news to newsrooms faster, allowing more papers to be printed faster, and delivering more papers in a timely fashion to readers in a wider area. The technological imperatives of the 1840s converted newspapers of the 1850s and 1860s—even in medium-sized towns—into mass-produced commodities with content that offered a same-day glimpse of the community and the nation.

Newspapers in John M. Wing's world during the two decades he grew to manhood and that employed him in upstate New York and Chicago in the 1860s were evolving from a handicraft trade to a mechanized industry, from political parties' handmaidens to independent commercial enterprises. So stunning were newspapers' growing reportorial prowess and technological reach between the 1840s and 1865 in the United States that some of the period's newspaper editors survive on the pages of history as giants—a generation of strident, innovative, and politically and socioculturally powerful voices such as Horace Greeley, James Gordon Bennett, Frederick Douglass, William Cullen Bryant, Henry J. Raymond, and the young Joseph Medill.[1]

The post-road network grew almost 15 percent during the 1840s to 178,672 miles in 1850, and the railroad system grew by more than 200 percent to 9,021 miles in 1850. Editors exchanged their newspapers free of charge through a postal system operating 18,417 postal offices in 1850, an increase of 36.7 percent during the 1840s.[2] Steam introduced dependable coastal shipping and, in 1840, predictable transatlantic crossings of Samuel Cunard's new side-paddle steamers carrying bundles of European newspapers to eastern U.S. newsrooms and crossing the Atlantic under almost any weather conditions in from fourteen to sixteen days.[3]

Before the 1840s, however, to transport news from place to place required storage on a medium—a correspondent's letter, a handwritten dispatch, a printed newspaper page, or the mind of a traveler. Not only is moving both the message and its medium bulky and time-consuming but an editor who relies on the postal service or a commercial transportation system receives his news no faster than his readers, making the newspaper a record of news already known rather than a messenger of new news.

Telegraphy separated the message from its physical medium, sending only the former at the speed of light throughout a network of wires, each impulse reaching the end of the wire only an instant after the telegrapher pressed his key. Appearing in 1844 as an experimental line between Washington, D.C., and Baltimore, the telegraph—or "lightning" as newspaper editors called it—steadily clicked out news dispatches in dot-and-dash Morse code as far as the lines could reach, eventually attaining thirty words per minute. "Special" telegraphic dispatches from correspondents to individual newspapers and the beginnings of the wire services followed in 1846.

By 1852, a rapidly expanding telegraph network had grown to 23,283 miles, connecting nearly five hundred cities and towns. The network stretched northeast to Halifax, Nova Scotia; north to Montreal and Quebec; northwest through Albany, Buffalo, and Chicago to Green Bay, Wisconsin; west to the Mississippi River in Illinois and beyond St. Louis to Kansas City, Missouri; southwest to New Orleans; and south to Savannah. Another ten thousand miles of telegraph line were under construction in 1852.[4]

Steam-driven flatbed printing presses first appeared in the United States in 1825, becoming the standard newspaper printing press in the 1840s wherever daily circulations exceeded one thousand. Meanwhile, as metropolitan dailies' circulations climbed to ten thousand and beyond in the early 1840s, the steam-powered type-revolving press—or "lightning press" as the Hoe Printing Press Company called its creation—appeared in 1847. Prior to 1850, press capacities rose from two hundred impressions per hour in 1800 to two thousand in 1825, to four thousand in 1832, and with Hoe's type-revolving press to as much as twenty thousand after 1847.[5]

Commanding such technological pull of news and push of product by 1850, newspaper publishers and editors began to sense the new commercial power of their enterprise overtaking its traditional political promise. Papers, although still political organs in 1850, could now begin to make money via speed and volume of production more easily than they could through reliance on the vagaries of election results, shifting political loyalties, and elitist party readership.

Journalism as a Mechanized Industry: the 1850s

A conversation on the ice-choked Hudson River at Albany, New York, in the winter of 1850–51 illustrates the changing complexion of newspapering in the United States at the time. Henry J. Raymond and George Jones were meeting a train at the railroad station on the other side of the river. After eight years on the staffs of two leading Whig papers, the *New York Tribune*, and the *Morning Courier and New York Enquirer*, and having just started his second term in the New York Legislature, Raymond was a politician-journalist in search of a newspaper to buy or create.

As they walked, Raymond and Jones, a political friend and an Albany banker, spoke about starting a Whig newspaper in New York City. Jones casually commented that Horace Greeley's *New York Tribune* had made a profit of sixty thousand dollars in 1850. A biographer described the impact this news had on Raymond:

> The information . . . seems to have been regarded with a feeling akin to awe,—for a clear profit of sixty thousand dollars for a single newspaper in one year was considered an immense success. . . . After further conversation, Mr. Raymond expressed his decided conviction that a new

paper could be started in New York, which would make as much money as the *Tribune*. . . .[6]

The newspaper that Raymond, Jones, and Jones's partner, E. B. Wesley, introduced in New York City on September 18, 1851, was the *Daily Times*, today's *New York Times*. Raymond's *Times* even copied the *Tribune*'s association system, a then revolutionary scheme for sharing investment, profit, risk, and protection with a handful of staffers and investors. Even though the plan appealed to Greeley's affinity for socialism, it was a magnificently capitalistic solution for floating a newspaper and profiting from its voyages.[7]

Imagine the editors of the two leading Whig newspapers in New York City in the early 1850s regularly proclaiming their Whiggery in print, dabbling in public office holding, raising significant capital, and making a profit. How thoroughly decadent and modern! Clearly, some newspapermen in New York City had discovered the secret to making journalism *both* politically and commercially potent. Here was commercialized[8] journalism's audition as the curtain was beginning to come down on "the dark ages of partisan journalism"[9] in the United States, as Frank Luther Mott described the party press.

With very few exceptions, from the founding of the republic in 1789 to the start of the Civil War in 1861, newspapers were openly allied with political parties—continually rallying the party faithful to vote for anointed candidates, vigorously debating the party's platforms, and using the party's prism to report the party's actions approvingly and to attack political enemies viciously in an endless vituperative quest for political advantage and government contracts.[10] Federalist or Whig papers, serving the political majority of the new nation's literate population, outnumbered the Democratic press until 1810,[11] after which partisan journalism of all American persuasions spread like a prairie fire to every frontier town and village where enough partisans could be found to support a party and its newspaper, neither viable locally without the other.

"In America there is scarcely a hamlet that has not its newspaper," observed Alexis de Tocqueville in the 1830s, continuing:

> All the political journals of the United States are, indeed, arrayed on the side of the administration or against it; but they attack and defend it in a thousand different ways. . . . The characteristics of the American journalist consist in an open and coarse appeal to the passions of his readers; he abandons principles to assail the character of individuals, to track them into private life and disclose all their weaknesses and vices.[12]

Rapidly growing, increasingly diverse metropolitan populations in New York City, Boston, Philadelphia, and Baltimore, however, by the 1840s nurtured less political strains of daily journalism. Mercantile newspapers, a fixture in metropolitan journalism for half a century, delivered a broad array of straight news and statistics about business, manufacturing, finances, market quotations, shipping, agriculture, and advertising of interest to the city's financial, investor, wholesaler, and retailer elites. Penny papers—some dating from the mid-1830s and most adopting a two-cent price within months of appearing—offered a variety of news, entertainment, and guidance, some of the news reporting tinged with sensationalism, for the rising middle class of clerks, young managers, and skilled tradespeople who increasingly migrated to cities, armed with some schooling and a Horatio Alger belief in hard work and striking it rich.

Partisan journalism by the 1850s was struggling to survive, challenged not so much by these urban journalism upstarts—whose audiences, after all, were different from the political papers'—but by the internal decay of the once brilliant and acerbic political newspapers themselves, passed on to less competent or less dedicated minds within a political system increasingly gridlocked by the intractable slavery question.

The *New York Daily Times* that Raymond and his colleagues launched in a sea with approximately fourteen other dailies[13] in September of 1851, was a penny paper, meaning that young boys noisily sold its copies for a penny to an identifiable slice of the city's population—in this case, middle-class Whigs who wanted their party's viewpoint corralled in editorial columns while news more professionally reported occupied most of the news columns. When the *Times* appeared, the city's six daily circulation leaders were all morning papers: three penny papers,[14] two party papers,[15] and one mercantile paper.[16]

Across all categories of journalism, the increase of dailies from 133 in 1850 to 387 in 1860 reflects both the continuing growth of the eastern press and the spread of the western press in the 1850s. Daily circulations nationally rose from 758,000 in 1850 to 1,478,000 in 1860. Even more striking, dailies and newspapers of all other publishing frequencies in the 1850s were in the midst of a century-long growth rate that exceeded national population growth. In 1800 there was one daily newspaper for evey 221,200 Americans, and despite the steady arrival of immigrants during the nineteenth century, in 1900 there was one daily newspaper for every 34,700 Americans.[17]

National expansion and migration along a broad westward-moving frontier in the 1840s and 1850s produced journalism instantly in its wake, offering local status and modest financial reward for the printer-editor who could move a press and type into the Midwest or onto the Great Plains and toward the great Rocky Mountains. Waves of immigrants, coupled with a steady westward flow of migrants along rivers, turnpikes, and growing rail and canal networks, poured hundreds of thousands of potential newspaper readers into the Midwest and West at midcentury.

In 1850 Chicago had six dailies.[18] Three were short-lived—the *Democrat Argus*, publishing only during 1850; the abolitionist *Western Citizen*, publishing from 1842 to 1854; and Alfred Dutch's *Commercial Advertiser*, Chicago's first mercantile paper, publishing from 1849 to 1853.[19] Three were substantial, continuing dailies—the *Chicago Democrat*, the *Daily Journal*, and the *Tribune*. All six were overtly partisan but also increasingly showed signs of serving the community beyond Chicago's political or economic elite.

The city's first newspaper, the *Chicago Weekly Democrat*, was founded by New Yorker and Jacksonian Democrat John Calhoun in 1833 after he brought type and a press from the East on a lake schooner, the same year Chicago was incorporated as a village. Two years later, the Whig weekly *Chicago American* appeared, reflecting the pattern so familiar in towns and villages throughout the United States of establishing a political paper in opposition to an existing one wherever partisan forces could muster sufficient numbers and financial support.

On November 14, 1836, "Long John" Wentworth, a rising political star who would represent Chicago in Congress for twelve years and twice be elected Chicago's mayor, purchased the *Democrat* from an ailing Calhoun and edited it for twenty-five years, turning it into a daily in 1840 and regularly defraying some of the paper's expenses from his private fortune. Not only was the *Democrat* its party's local mouthpiece until the mid-1850s, but the paper benefited by local government contracts and close ties, through Wentworth, to several local private companies.

Wentworth sold the *Democrat* to the Republican *Chicago Tribune* in the summer of 1861,[20] Wentworth's biographer, quoting him, observing:

> Admittedly an "old fogy" paper, a relic of Chicago's simpler and cruder past, [the *Democrat*] was holding its patrons with difficulty and losing money every week. Urban journalism had become a big business and Long John readily conceded that the city had outgrown his "ability to keep up with it in the newspaper line."[21]

The *American* became a daily in 1839 but disappeared in 1842, when Chicago Whigs withdrew their support. It was followed by the *Chicago Express*, a campaign paper supporting Henry Clay for president, but Clay's defeat in 1844 derailed the *Express*, clearing the way for a more broadly based Whig paper, the *Daily Journal*, which Richard Wilson founded in 1844.

Because James Kelly, the owner of the literary weekly *Gem of the Prairie*, was interested in 1847 in redirecting his weekly away from essays and toward news, he found backers to help him establish a Chicago daily that would provide news copy for the weekly. Kelly and two partners introduced the *Chicago Tri-*

bune on June 10, 1847.[22] In an act of the tail wagging the dog, the *Tribune* converted the *Gem of the Prairie* into its Sunday edition in 1852.[23]

Although the *Tribune* was nominally Free-Soiler in the beginning, its owners wistfully outlined in the paper's first prospectus a nonpartisan mission:

> Our views, in all probability, will sometimes be coincident with the conservatives; sometimes we may be found in the ranks of the radicals; but shall at all times be faithful to humanity—to the whole of humanity—without regard to race, sectional divisions, party lines, or parallels of latitude or longitude.[24]

The paper at times leaned toward straight Whig principles, at others evincing a Know-Nothing sympathy or Native American extremism.

In 1853 new owners introduced a strong preference for religion and temperance, and in June of 1855 Joseph Medill and Dr. Charles Ray, another set of new owners, cut short the *Tribune*'s flights into extremism. With debate over slavery heating up and the new Republican party rising from Whig ashes to denounce slavery, Medill and Ray offered this Republican prospectus on September 24, 1855:

> Believing that the spread of Liberty, and not of Bondage, is the saving principle of the Republic, the *Tribune* has enlisted in the ranks of National Republicans, not for a campaign, but during the war, believing that slavery or involuntary servitude is inconsistent with all principles, civil or religious. . . .[25]

Little wonder that on June 5, 1865, the day after he arrived in Chicago, Republican Jack Wing first called at the offices of the city's leading Republican dailies—the *Journal* and the week-old *Republican*, before having a tryout at the *Tribune*, where he "received rather a cold shoulder."

Strong, passionate editorials were a hallmark of Chicago newspapers until the 1960s. During the Civil War, the *Tribune*'s Republicanism and Wilbur F. Storey's Democratic Chicago

Times roared at each other every day. While many eastern metropolitan dailies began confining their politics increasingly to their editorial columns and some political and election coverage in the 1850s, party and political benefactors still invariably defined journalism in the West. Local politicians and the party faithful called the tune to which midwestern editors danced.

No clearer example of this exists than Chicago's press and popular reaction to the 1854 compromise Kansas-Nebraska Act, which allowed residents of these two territories to decide for themselves whether they would be free soil or slaveholding. After a bitter debate, Congress passed the measure, which contradicted the promise of the Missouri Compromise of 1820 that all territory in the Louisiana Purchase north of the southern border of Missouri would be free soil. Illinois Senator Stephen A. Douglas, author of the Kansas-Nebraska Act, came home after his triumph to find that he had no newspaper support for the act and faced considerable public resentment as well.

Wentworth, cautious about his political status in a Chicago seemingly full of Free-Soilers, steered his *Democrat* toward the Free-Soil viewpoint in 1854 after being the voice of the Democratic party for sixteen years. "Every Chicago newspaper condemned the Kansas-Nebraska Act," stated Robin L. Einhorn. "Not only did the Whig *Tribune* and *Journal* oppose Douglas, but the three Democratic papers, *Democrat, Press*, and *Staats-Zeitung*, also repudiated his leadership."

Realizing that, in keeping with the political necessities of the day, he now needed a paper of his own in Chicago, Douglas in August of 1854 persuaded James W. Sheahan to come from Washington, D.C., and establish the *Chicago Times*, which he did that November, with Douglas financing the venture directly from his own pocket.[26] "A year later," Einhorn added, "Douglas men added the *National Demokrat* to compete with the *Staats-Zeitung*."[27] Douglas continued to subsidize this version of the Democratic party voice in Chicago during the late 1850s. The *Times* conducted a blistering anti-Lincoln and proslavery editorial assault as the Civil War approached.

This *Chicago Times* was the paper that Storey purchased on June 4, 1861, after an eight-year reign as editor of the Democratic *Detroit Free Press*.[28] During the Civil War, the *Times* was the leading copperhead paper, a Northern paper that sympathized with Southern secessionists or opposed emancipation. Dripping with irony, Jack Wing, a pro-Lincoln Republican, writes in his diary on June 13, 1865, "Whoever thought that I should be hard at work on the greatest copperhead paper in the whole country." And on July 26 Wing writes, "Wrote an article on 'Negro Immigration' in which I said many things against my belief, now that I am selling my brains to a copperhead paper."

* * *

Despite the telegraph and its "lightning" news, life in newsrooms of the 1850s and 1860s was not as hectic as it would become when typewriters and telephones began to appear there in the 1880s. One high point was the arrival of the daily bundle of exchange newspapers, which presented editors with a panoply of news stories and essays to reprint. The editor or his managing editor would circle, clip, or tear a selected story from the exchanges, write a headline in available white space or on a separate slip of paper and attach it to the clipping with a straight pin. The whole thing was then sent to the shop to be set in type. Stories were selected for reprinting because they contained local interest, an unusual or sensational angle, or some political significance.

Although Jack Wing notes occasionally the writing of long stories on deadline for the *Times*, the news-gathering pace was ordinarily leisurely in his day. "Item gatherers" or "assistant editors," as reporters were occasionally called, would work their beats by interviewing sources, visiting government and police offices, rushing to disasters, and attending meetings and court sessions. In most respects, Wing's daily out-of-the-office news-gathering routine of observing and interviewing was quite similar to that of today's city reporters.

After decades of emphasizing foreign and nonlocal domestic news in large part because local news was already known to local readers, metropolitan newspaper editors in the 1830s began gathering and printing local police and court news. As cities grew beyond residents' personal experience, newspapers found that local news was indeed news to local readers. In New York City, for example, with populations of 515,547 in 1850 and 805,651 in 1860,[29] a newspaper needed reporters to cover such "beats" or "runs" as police, fire, courts, business, financial, local government, harbor, shipping, features, and general assignment.

The *New York Tribune*, for example, employed twelve editors and reporters and bought articles from seventeen correspondents in 1850. A mere four years later, the same paper had ten associate editors, fourteen reporters, and thirty-eight correspondents. To orchestrate a growing news staff, publishers in the 1840s introduced the position of a "managing editor," who eventually acquired administrative duties and in the 1850s yielded oversight of local coverage to "chief reporters" or "city editors."[30]

In smaller cities such as Chicago, two or three reporters, in addition to a publisher-editor, a chief editor, and a couple of assistant editors, adequately met reporting needs in the 1850s. Although city editors arrived in such places in the mid- or late-1860s, the *Chicago Tribune*'s historian first names an "editor of local news" in connection with staff changes in 1855.[31] This was somewhat ahead of other western communities, but Chicago, with a population of 29,963 in 1850, 60,000 in 1853, and 109,200 in 1860,[32] had jumped from twenty-fifth to ninth largest U.S. city during the 1850s.

Although we know that the *Chicago Times* was emphasizing local news immediately after Storey bought the paper in 1861[33] and had a city editor, James H. Goodsell, as early as 1863, we do not know how many reporters the *Times* had while Jack Wing was on the staff in 1865. In describing his own introduction to the *Times* in September of 1863, Franc B. Wilkie, however, offered a glimpse of the news office Wing worked in and the first-day jitters that Wing may have felt as a new employee of the demanding Mr. Storey:

I received a letter from James H. Goodsell, city editor of the Chicago *Times*, in which he stated that he was instructed by Mr. Storey to offer me a position as assistant editor on his staff. . . .

The clamor about Storey was so great, his reported abuse of his employes so wide-spread, the assertions as to his open treason so emphatic and universal that it was with considerable hesitation that I responded affirmatively to Goodsell's letter. . . . I was an unfaltering Democrat [but] did not care to incur the odium of being a "copperhead," a "rebel sympathizer," "secessionist," and all the other terms of contumely and opprobrium which I knew association with Storey's paper would necessarily inflict on me. . . .

Goodsell . . . was a tall, slender, handsome young fellow, with a bright face, active motions, and very agreeable in his manners. As I soon discovered, although barely out of Ann Arbor University, he was already a valuable man in his profession—alert, capable, vigilant and untiring. . . .

I re-entered the editorial room at nine a.m. on the agreed morning [in September of 1863]. A small swarthy man with jet-black hair, large, very dark eyes and a face full of intensity, sat at a small table glancing over a newspaper. We made ourselves acquainted. He was, he said, Mr. M. L Hopkins, senior assistant editor. . . . For several years thereafter we occupied tables in the same room. . . .

I took possession of the table pointed out to me by Mr. Hopkins and . . . studied the room. It was spacious on the floor, high as to ceiling, lighted dimly from the dirty windows of the light shaft [at the rear of the building]. There was a book-case, with glass doors, containing perhaps one or two hundred books of a very miscellaneous kind, and piled in a corner were great numbers of black-coated official reports, and litters of newspaper.

There was a carpet on the floor, a sofa on one side, all of which substantially comprised the furniture of the editorial room.

Probably at no time in my journalistic experience was I in so great a quandary, so perplexed, so undecided what to do and how to do it. . . .

> I pondered over the problem for a long time. Should it be something on the war question; a political essay; a smart denunciation of some military commander? . . .
>
> It was an hour or more after I had taken my seat, when my eye lighted on a brief [newspaper] account of an outrage perpetrated on the inmates of a charitable institution for the care of poor children. Here was the sought-for theme! Something to awaken the sympathy of the tender-hearted; to arouse righteous indignation; to stir the pulses of the public. It contained pathetic elements; it involved pity; it was just the class of craft needed with which to embark on unknown waters.
>
> I wrote up the subject in my best style; I was poetical without being "sloppy," indignant without being brutal in expression and Christian-like in my demand for the punishment of the guilt of the culpable managers.[34]

Wilkie cleverly and correctly determined what kind of story would be right at home in the *Times*'s news columns, and when he looked for his items in the next day's paper, "they were there, just as I had written them, punctuation and all." Wilkie remained with the *Times* until 1884, becoming Storey's closest associate on the paper.

The *Times*'s newsroom Wilkie describes above was at 74 Randolph Street, between Dearborn and State streets in a three-story building, measuring sixty by one hundred feet. The paper had moved into this new building on November 5, 1861, with its new Hoe four-cylinder type-revolving press, and remained there until it occupied a news plant on Dearborn Street, near Madison Street, in September of 1866.[35] The Randolph location was where Jack Wing labored on the *Times* from June to December of 1865.

Most journalists in the early and middle nineteenth century had spent some time as printer's devils, the older editors having had their introduction to the news office as apprentices in print shops, hauling paper to the presses and washing type, later graduating to printing papers at the press and setting news stories into type. By the 1840s, some younger metropolitan editors had high-school, even college, educations, but many reporters and most of the old editors still had learned newswriting style and news judgment by setting news copy into type—one character at a time, line by line, story by story, day after day.

Like journeyman printers, who after completing their apprenticeships moved from shop to shop in search of agreeable working conditions, nineteenth-century reporters were nomads, jumping to another paper in search of better prospects or because they had been fired on whim or for mistakes they had made. A common way for reporters to improve their prospects was to migrate from small communities where they had learned the trade to larger towns and cities where the pay was better and the opportunities for reporting were more exciting and interesting. Turnover in newsrooms was endless.

Most reporters entered the field in their teens. For some, writing about other people's misery or machinations was tolerable—a way of surmounting a lack of education or bad family circumstances—and for others it was voyeuristic, exhilarating, or economically expedient. The former eventually moved on to other work by the time they were forty years old, but the latter likely stayed and became editors. Reporters wrote their stories in pencil or pen on short sheets of paper, many in their haste writing in the style used by telegraphers to record dispatches from the rapid clicks of telegraph sounders—that is, using a continuous line to form the words without breaking for spaces and interrupting the line only between lines of copy. Again, straight pins held the several pages, of "takes" or "adds" of a story together.

Nineteenth-century reporters were thought of collectively as rude, coarse drunkards. Because journalism is always a buyer's market at the bottom of the ladder, young reporters were poorly paid and ordinarily compensated by the line or the inch. Beginning city reporters received from $5 to $10 a week in cash, usually paid on Saturdays. Industrious reporters, in the days before concerns about conflicts of interest, augmented their income by turning news stories into freelance articles or pamphlets or accepting small sums for favorably mentioning a person, product, or company in a news story, called a "puff" in the business.[36]

The majority of dailies—including Chicago's *Republican, Times,* and *Tribune*—were morning papers, meaning that their copy deadlines were somewhere between midnight and 2 A.M. and the papers were printed after 2 or 3 A.M. for sale by about 6 A.M. While the staff's clipped and handwritten copy flowed continuously into the composing room all day and up to final deadline, all Associated Press (AP) wire copy before the Civil War arrived in Chicago newsrooms between 11 and 11:30 P.M. and was usually the last copy set in type.

By the mid-1850s, the AP had emerged, for the moment at least, as the nation's only news-gathering agency, availing itself of the rapidly expanding telegraphic network to send its daily news reports to newspapers well beyond the Mississippi River and into Texas. Headquartered in New York City and a partnership of the seven leading dailies of that city, the AP telegraphed its news report in code to guard against poaching and to keep transmission costs down. Depending on the amount of news, the report was one to two newspaper columns of stories.[37] The volume and quality of the AP report would become serious issues for Chicago publishers during the Civil War.

Conditions in newsrooms were messy and bleak, but in the composing rooms they were downright dangerous, with compositors handling type made mostly of lead and breathing air laden with lead and printing ink fumes. Compositors stood at their type cases fifteen to nineteen hours a day, setting stories into type and being paid, in Chicago in 1854, thirty cents per thousand ems or about $1.67 per hour.[38] Until typesetting machines arrived in the 1880s, stories were set in foundry type, letter by letter, with each line of type the same length as all the others so that the type would stay firmly locked in place on the press. The *New York Times* began life in the fall of 1851 with eighteen compositors who filled four modern-sized broadsheet pages with type each day.[39]

Compositors set type generally without having to read the type. Even though newspaper columns were ordinarily set in very small type (5- to 8-point type, as compared with 12-point type today), typesetters knew where the characters were in their cases and could set type almost with their eyes closed, a notch on the side of each piece of type telling their fingers whether that letter was sitting right side up in the typesetter's composing stick.[40]

Ventilation and illumination, the latter needed primarily to read newspaper clippings and reporters' scrawls, were terrible. As newspapers in their newly mechanized state replaced their old buildings with new newspaper factories of their own design, they located their compositors on the top floor under a glass roof that let in light in the daytime. Augustus Maverick explains that in the *New York Times'* new building, for example, designed for newspaper production and occupied in May of 1858, "the composing-room . . . takes up the entire [top] floor. . . . The ceiling is pierced by skylights and ventilators, opening to the roof. . . . A steam hoistway extends to the [pressroom] vaults below the pavement, for the purpose of raising and lowering the [printing] plates."[41] After sunset compositors relied on candles or oil lamps in the 1850s. (Gas lamps began to appear in newspaper offices after the Civil War, and electric lights appeared in metropolitan newsrooms in the 1880s.)

The work of typesetting was so demanding, requiring such skill and concentration, that compositors and pressmen had made several attempts in eastern cities to organize a union before December of 1850, when the National Typographical Union appeared.[42] Typographers obtained a charter for Local No. 16 of the union in June of 1852, one of the first unions in Chicago. Membership reached 142, or roughly one-third of the typesetters and printers in Cook County, in 1860. The *Chicago Times*, receiving tacit support from the *Chicago Tribune*, would not recognize the union. When the printers struck the paper in April 1864, Storey trained women to set type in a building at some distance from the *Times* office. On September 9, 1864, he marched forty female compositors into the *Times* shop and locked the union out. Organized labor never gained a foothold at the *Times* as long as Storey lived.[43]

Most dailies in the 1850s were four pages—one sheet folded in half. While New York City dailies had expanded to eight pages by the 1860s, Chicago's *Times* and *Tribune* both remained four-page sheets throughout the Civil War. By the 1830s, most dailies were printed on steam-driven flatbed (also known as cylinder) presses that moved type for two newspaper pages (either pages one and four or two and three), locked in place on a table, called the bed, that rolled back and forth under inking rollers and a pressure cylinder. The cylinder gripped a single sheet of paper at the top of its revolution, carrying it around to be printed at the bottom as the inked type passed under the cylinder, in sync with the cylinder's motion. This press, depending on the model and power source, could print between two thousand and four thousand impressions per hour. Developed in England in the second decade of the nineteenth century, flatbed presses first appeared in the United States in 1825.[44]

As eastern metropolitan dailies' circulations reached beyond ten thousand, the Hoe Printing Press Company responded in 1847 with the type-revolving press that tightly gripped the type for two newspaper pages on a six-and-a-half-foot-diameter central cylinder. As the type turned on this cylinder, it was inked and then printed on handfed sheets that passed between the type and pressure cylinders arranged around the central type cylinder. The type-revolving press could have anywhere from two to ten pressure cylinders arranged around the type cylinder, each pressure cylinder capable of printing about two thousand impressions per hour. The press could thus print from four thousand to twenty thousand impressions per hour.[45]

As with the flatbed press, the type-revolving press printed on only one side of a sheet (two newspaper pages) at a time, requiring pressmen either to change the type on a press halfway through the pressrun or to run two presses simultaneously, one for pages one and four and the other for pages two and three. Newspapers in the 1850s still used rag paper, made as separate sheets that were fed into printing presses one sheet at a time. After ten years of experiments, presses that could print on both sides of a continuous sheet of paper from a roll appeared in the 1870s.[46]

The *Philadelphia Ledger* installed the first type-revolving press in March 1847. The next year, New York's *Sun*, with forty thousand daily circulation, and *Herald,* with 17,280 daily circulation, installed type-revolver presses, and the *Sun* acquired another type-revolver the next year.

Likewise in other cities, daily circulations determined press needs. The *Chicago Tribune,* for example, with a daily circulation of twelve hundred in December 1851, used a flatbed press powered by an old black Canadian pony tramping on a revolving platform. Seven months later, the *Tribune* added another flatbed press.[47] In 1861 the *Tribune,* with a daily circulation of 16,451, acquired its first Hoe type-revolving press, a line etching of which was featured in the paper's nameplate in the early 1860s. In 1864 the *Tribune* installed an eight-cylinder type-revolving press.[48] The *Chicago Times* installed its first type-revolving press, with four pressure cylinders, in November 1861, when the paper moved to new quarters at 74 Randolph Street.[49]

Most of the resulting newspapers in the 1840s devoted their front pages to long essays, reprints of stories from other newspapers, short business-card advertisements, or one-column ads that ranged from one to four inches in depth. Page four contained more ads and a variety of business, shipping, stock, produce, and weather news. These two pages were usually printed first. Pages two and three contained the latest wire service dispatches, local news stories, and the editorials—ordinarily in the left-hand columns of page two with the lead editorials commenting on that day's news.

Indicative of the growing commercialization of newspapering in the 1850s, the entire front page of the *New York Times*'s first issue in September 1851 was devoted to news from Europe and news items from New York City and Brooklyn.[50] And as secession and the Civil War became reality, dailies increasingly put their war news on page one. Chicago's *Tribune* and *Times* followed opposite paths on makeup during the Civil War. The *Tribune*'s nine- and later ten-column front pages devoted an average of three columns to a news summary and clips from other newspapers, two or three columns to "The Latest News" by telegraph, two columns of specials to the *Tribune,* and three or four columns to "New Advertisements." The

Civil War *Tribune* was a strikingly large paper, measuring 21 inches wide by 27 ½ inches deep.

The *Times* used an older makeup pattern on its eight-column front pages during the Civil War, devoting three columns to "New Advertisements" and five to special dispatches and letters to the *Times* and clippings from other newspapers. "The Latest" news by telegraph, Storey's editorials, and the beginnings of several columns of "The City" stories and briefs (that continued on page three) were on page two. The Civil War size of the *Times* resembled the broadsheet size of modern dailies.

Newspaper body type in the 1850s was only 5 to 8 points in size—that is fourteen and one-half to nine lines of type per column inch, respectively. There were no photographs, infrequently a portrait or a sketch or a map rendered as a line etching, no advertisements beyond one column wide and a few inches deep. The most frequent illustrations were stock cuts of ships, merchandise, or commercial symbols inserted for a fee in advertisements.

Headlines—even during the Civil War and for President Lincoln's assassination—were one column wide, although an item of sufficient news value would have several one-column heads, each devoted to a different aspect of the story, stacked one on top of another, and sometimes reaching one-third or more down the column. Stories continued from the bottom of one column to the top of the next (or from one page to the next) without a headline separating the continued story from the top of the page.

While the ability of a printing press to exert even pressure across a printed page had determined the size of the newspaper pages previously, the new presses in the 1830s and 1840s were designed to print standard-size broadsheet newspaper pages, very close to the 14- by 21-inch newspapers still published at the end of the twentieth century. Six two-and-a-half-inch columns were fairly standard in the 1850s, again like the layout of late-twentieth-century pages.[51]

Journalism During the Civil War: 1861–1865

"With the first hostile gun at Fort Sumter, the old Democratic

Party which started into life with Jefferson in 1789, tumbled to pieces, and ceased to be a power," said Frederic Hudson, for many years the managing editor of the Democratic *New York Herald*.[52] The Civil War dissolved much of the prewar network of Democratic newspapers in the North and forced the rest, such as the *New York Herald*, to downplay or modify their proslavery sympathies. Only a handful of Northern Democratic papers stood by their prosecession, antiemancipation principles—including such infamous copperhead papers as the *New York Daily News* and the *Chicago Times*.

Meanwhile, Republicanism, which in the mid-1850s emerged after several antislavery meetings in midwestern states, replacing the waning Whig party, gathered strength with the election of Abraham Lincoln and the coming crusade for emancipation, and resonated in the editorials of such papers as the *New York Tribune* and the *Chicago Tribune*.

Old habits die hard. Politics would, of course, survive the Civil War, receiving daily transfusions in the editorial columns of American newspapers after 1865, but secession and the Civil War were the last hurrah for the old party press movement, in which "we" and "our boys" in newspaper stories referred to the Confederacy or the Union troops as they had referred to the Democratic or Republican faithful before the war.

As sectionalism deteriorated into hostilities in 1861 at Sumter and the first Bull Run, metropolitan newspaper editors, sensing the journalistic obligation and financial opportunity of reporting this crusade to anxious readers back home, began flooding the battlefields and capitals with correspondents who poked into officers' tents and government's offices, clamoring for a better view and an earlier word of victory or defeat. Even though quickly brought under military control in both the North and South, the extensive 1861 telegraph system was the conduit for many of the important news dispatches that reached newsrooms from the front, the rest coming by mail.

Some New York City papers spared no expense covering the war, stationing at times as many as twenty correspondents on various battlefields. The *New York Herald* had the most correspondents—more than sixty during the course of the war—followed by New York City's *Times* and *Tribune*, the numbers changing seasonally and in response to the level of military engagement. A few other newspapers also employed many correspondents, or "specials" as they were called, notably the *Boston Journal, New York Evening Post, Philadelphia Press, Cincinnati Gazette*, and *Chicago Tribune*.

By one estimate, roughly five hundred reporters covered the war for Northern papers at one time or another, about two hundred of which were regulars, spending significant periods of time in the field.[53] J. Cutler Andrews, the leading scholar on Civil War journalism, identified three hundred forty-three correspondents for Northern papers and ninety-six Confederate correspondents, twenty of the latter writing for more than one news organization during the war.[54] "Probably no great war has ever been so thoroughly covered by eye-witness correspondents as the American Civil War," observed historian Mott.[55] Andrews listed twenty-eight full- and part-time war correspondents for Chicago dailies: fifteen for the *Tribune*, seven for the *Times*, four for the *Journal*, and two for the *Post*. These were small contingents, compared with New York City's dailies, but respectable numbers for a city with barely more than one hundred thousand population in 1860 and with eight daily newspapers.[56]

War coverage was a tour de force for editors and their correspondents, a chance to report the sights and sounds of this spellbinding life-and-death struggle between two sections of the same nation. "The roar, the bursting bombs, the impression of magnificent power," as Whitelaw Reid described it in his news account of Pickett's fateful charge at Gettysburg, "'all the glory visible, all the horror of the fearful field concealed,' a nation's existence trembling as the clangor of those iron monsters swayed the balance—it was a sensation for a century!"[57]

As if the "sensation" of war were not enough, the papers were also filled with rumors, fabrications, and exaggerations, much of it, however, accidental or based on faulty sources. And part of the blame for this rested with editors' low ethical standards. "The editors were more likely to censure a reporter," said Andrews, "for being scooped by an enterprising rival than for including items of doubtful authenticity."[58] Colorful, descriptive, emotional, stark, and always sectionally patriotic coverage was the norm on both sides.

And while the leading metropolitan newspapers boosted their circulations and fortunes with "specials" from battlefields, the rest of the U.S. press had to settle for reprints from other newspapers and the meager AP stories and bulletins based on government dispatches. One cannot escape the conclusion that because several of AP's seven New York City partners were big players in the war coverage, AP was relegated to a secondary role during the war.

In the Midwest, the quality and length of the AP news report, which had been simmering issues throughout the 1850s, reached the boiling point during the Civil War. Daniel H. Craig, AP's general agent in New York City in the 1850s, "was the boss and dictator," recalled the *Chicago Tribune*'s Medill in 1896. Craig

> had a short and effective way of enforcing discipline and maintaining his authority. If any of us grumbled at the lateness of receiving his news, or its quality, or talked back to his autocracy, he cut us off, stopped our news, and after we had begged his pardon and promised never to repeat our offense, he would let up, but fine us to the amount of the cost of the news as if we had received it.[59]

At the start of the war, a meager fifteen hundred-word news report per day went west from Buffalo and Pittsburgh into Chicago. The regular report was delivered to midwestern papers between 11 and 11:30 P.M., often too early to include important late-breaking news from the East. The western editors in 1861 negotiated an additional midnight report of one thousand words and then gained a three hundred-word report, and then another five hundred words of news, as a midday "postscript" for the evening editions of the morning paper and for the handful of evening papers.

As the war dragged on with AP's quality improving, the midwestern editors began holding secret annual discussions about their mutual concerns, leading on March 21, 1865, to incorporation of the Western Associated Press, a regional wire service bounded by the Appalachian Mountains, Canada, Colorado, and the Ohio and Missouri rivers. In 1866 the Western AP ratified bylaws and gained complete equality with the AP in New York City.

During early, secret meetings, some western editors expressed fear that any effort at organizing might permanently cost them their all-important AP news report. It would have been an act of supreme journalistic courage to organize the Western AP were it not for the fact that the actual act came a few weeks after the war was over. Although the *Tribune*'s Medill took the lead in this regional insurrection,[60] Chicago had five AP newspapers in 1865: *Illinois Staats-Zeitung, Journal, Post, Times,* and *Tribune*.[61]

The unity among otherwise politically warring Chicago newspapers evident in their confrontation with the New York AP was missing, however, when it came to Union war policy. A notable incident of division within the journalistic ranks involved the *Chicago Times*. Storey biographer Justin E. Walsh noted that history's verdict on Storey is based exclusively on the editor's Civil War copperhead politics, on being "a blackguard, a traitor. . . . The utter viciousness of Storey's crusade against Lincoln" and the subsequent assassination of Lincoln, observed Walsh, reinforced history's verdict against Storey and did "violence to the truth and an injustice to the editor."[62]

Walsh argued that up to September 1862, Storey supported the federal government and Lincoln after his inauguration, even "defend[ing] Lincoln vociferously against the almost daily assaults of the President's own partisans."[63] Wilkie, who joined the *Times* as an assistant editor in September 1863, confirmed that Storey "favored a war for the preservation of the Union."[64] But Walsh failed to note that the "almost daily assaults of the President's own partisans" urged a reluctant Lincoln to issue the Emancipation Proclamation, freeing slaves in all areas of the former United States. Emancipation to Storey meant economic ruin in both the South and the North.[65] On September 22, 1862, Lincoln issued a preliminary emancipation proclamation, stating that unless the rebel states returned to the Union by January 1, 1863, he would declare all slaves forever free. That month Storey shed any vestiges of support for Lincoln.

In August 1862, meanwhile, Illinois governor Richard Yates had written U.S. Secretary of War Edwin M. Stanton, reporting the "urgent and almost unanimous demand from local citizens" that the *Times* be suppressed. As a show of contempt for the paper's politics, the Chicago Board of Trade had excluded the *Times* reporters from its offices, and the Galena and Chicago Union Railroad forbade sale of the *Times* on its trains.[66]

Finally on June 2, 1863, General Ambrose Burnside, Union commander of the military district that included Illinois, ordered Union troops to seize the paper and suspend publication. The order read: "On account of the repeated expression of disloyal and incendiary statements, the publication of the newspaper known as the Chicago *Times* is hereby suppressed."[67] At 4 A.M. on June 3, Union soldiers marched into the *Times* offices, halting publication. By noon "sane-minded citizens of both parties," according to historian Bessie Louise Pierce,[68] had petitioned Lincoln to free the paper. Even Jack Wing, who was still in New York in 1863, wrote an article decrying the suppression.

After the "Democratic ward bosses had worked the riverfront all day [June 3] to ensure that a healthy number of Irish dock hands were present," according to Theodore J. Karamanski, a crowd estimated at twenty thousand assembled at courthouse square by 8 P.M. to demand revocation of the order.[69] Some of the speakers also vehemently attacked the gloating *Tribune,* which supported the order. The paper was forced to post armed guards around its shop in fear of mob attack. Lincoln revoked the order on June 4, and the *Times* resumed publishing on June 5.[70] The incident ensured a place for Storey and his paper in the history books, said Walsh, as a "damned Copperhead" and a "treason sheet."[71] Perhaps, but the suspension boosted the paper's fortunes with its traditional lower-class immigrant readership. Bad reputation or not, the *Times* was one of Chicago's circulation leaders for many years, always able to attract attention with its saucy, sensational coverage.

"Journalism in the Civil War," observed Michael Schudson, "was not so much different as bigger, more prominent, and as people anxiously followed campaigns that involved their husbands and brothers and sons, more important to ordinary people."[72] In the war's aftermath, "certain phenomena of change are noticeable" in newspapering, said Mott, especially "the growth of independence from party bonds, the growth of feature material in the place of long political disquisitions, and the accelerated expansion . . . of midwestern journalism."[73]

A crashing five-day crescendo of news embracing victory at Appomattox Court House and the assassination of Lincoln gave the northern press a final rush of news and a spike in circulations that left editors wondering whether postwar reunification and the trial of assassins would sustain the high readership levels that they enjoyed during the war. How could a newspaper's editor maintain his news readership and political leadership when AP and "special" dispatches no longer arrived daily giving eyewitness accounts of glorious victory and ignominious defeat, of survival and death on the battlefield?

Put simply, he could not if he decided to return to the prewar days of partisan journalism. Success would henceforth arise from focusing on local socioeconomic (especially crime) coverage, confining political comment increasingly to editorial columns, harnessing the expanding financial support from burgeoning postwar retailing, and dressing up pages in bolder typography.

While many of his colleagues learned these lessons painfully by trial and error—or failing to learn them, fell by the wayside—Storey knew these principles instinctively, and despite being a political spoiler in Republican territory, he served his laboring readers' tastes unashamedly and with precision. Wilkie described the postwar, pre-1871 *Times* reporting as follows:

> Scandals in private life, revolting details from the evidence taken in police-court trials, imaginary liaisons of a filthy character, reeked, seethed like a hell's broth in the *Times'* cauldrons, and made a stench in the nostrils of decent people. All this was done with a purpose: it was to

> attract attention to the paper, to secure notoriety, advertising and circulation. . . . It was a feast fitted only for the tastes and appetites of vultures and carrion-loving vermin.[74]

"Debauchery and sensationalism, however, represented only one side of *Chicago Times*," said Walsh, asserting that Storey, "more than any other editor in the region, mastered the divergent possibilities that the war opened for American journalism." The *Times* "exaggerat[ed] the available news with a melodramatic flair under headlines intended to keep the attention of the sensation-fed public of the war years," stated Walsh, and it "broadened the scope of news matter, [adding] variety, human appeal and general readability."[75]

"The only time Storey ever beat a retreat was in August of 1865," reported Karamanski, when one of the *Times* reporters portrayed, quoting the story, "shanties, the filth of the streets, the crime, brawls and drunkenness of the Irish in our midst."[76] That reporter was Jack Wing and his story, entitled "Squatter Settlements," an exposé of the Kilgubblin Irish ghetto, "touched to the quick of the *Times'* most loyal readership," Karamanski continued. Storey "was abject in his apologies to the Irish and stemmed the tide of subscription cancellations by heaping unrestrained praise on the sons and daughters of Erin in the weeks that followed."[77]

The practices of reporters after the Civil War reflected the changing newspaper business. Newspaper reporters' desire to be published, to make money, and to gain attention mirrored their employers' desire, as Wilkie phrased it, for "notoriety, advertising and circulation." Lambert A. Wilmer's 1859 *Our Press Gang; or, A Complete Exposition of the Corruptions and Crimes of the American Newspapers* indicted the antebellum editor for grasping and wielding too much power and influence, leaving reporters' practices for the most part beyond his critical sphere. After the Civil War, criticism of the press focused more and more on reporters' methods, which, by emphasizing sensationalism, increasingly defined news as intrusive and marketable.

Hazel Dicken-Garcia, noting that "the bulk of nineteenth-century press discussion" of standards came after the Civil War, listed five themes in criticism of the press that gained strength after 1865: (1) profit seeking; (2) serving advertising more than news functions; (3) invading privacy, which "came to dominate criticism during the 1880s"; (4) sensationalizing, which became a prevalent critical theme by 1870 and included reporting of "crime, sex, violence, and gossip"; and (5) overemphasizing the trivial or unimportant.[78] The *Chicago Times* surely was a proud contributor to this postwar bill of particulars.

Of especial interest on this list, however, is "serving advertising more than news functions," a territory shared by editors and reporters. The commercializing of newspapering after 1865 made editors and publishers increasingly dependent on retail advertising for their revenue and cooperative with advertisers by including "reading notices," which are advertisments in the form of news stories placed in news columns. "Major American newspapers," reported Gerald J. Baldasty, "had standardized rates for these notices."

"Puffs" during the nineteenth century were many reporters' opportunity to make extra money. Any journalist, for a few dollars, could insert an approving mention of a product or store in an otherwise legitimate news story. Reporters might be solicited for their puff or might offer it. In addition to covering the news, a reporter out on the beat found that he had many opportunities to pocket extra money for inserting puffs. Regular advertisers were instructed by ad agencies to seek the puffs free from newspapers, and some publishers routinely would insert puffs for a fee from firms whose advertisements already appeared in the newspaper.

Reporters could also get free accommodations from hotels and railroads on basis of the proposition, as one advertising journal put it, that "nothing will ever be said about a railroad by a reporter that will injure it, if the railroad has made the reporter its friend."[79] Jack Wing's diary indicates that he was no stranger to free passes and puffs in his brief career as a newspaper reporter.

The newspaper industry of 1865 underwent rapid change as publishers tried to retain Civil War strength with new postwar content. While it was a fearful time for publishers, it was an unsettling time for reporters who were treading for the line that separated marketable sensationalism from wretched excess, libel, and stepping on the wrong toes. The possibilities for news reporting were endless in Chicago—a raucous frontier city of one hundred thousand in 1860 heading toward a bustling commercial center of three hundred thousand in 1870. Former journalist Hudson observed in 1873 that since the Civil War,

> New organs of public opinion sprung into existence. New papers in the form of the Independent Press, new men for political leaders, new sets of carpet-baggers, and new parties made their entrée . . . with fresh ideas and fresh vigor and have taken their place in the world of action. These new elements are to control the destinies of the United States for the next fifty years.[80]

This was the newspaper world that John M. Wing encountered when he arrived in Chicago in June of 1865.

Richard A. Schwarzlose
Northwestern University

Notes

1. As this generation of editors began to fade from the scene around 1870, biographers and historians, sensing a changing of the guard, applied their literary talents to these men. Examples of leading editors of the 1840s and 1850s and literature about them are *New York Journal of Commerce*'s Gerard Hallock by his son, William H. Hallock, *Life of Gerard Hallock: Thirty-three Years Editor of the New York Journal of Commerce* (New York: Oakley, Mason, 1869); *Washington* (D.C.) *Globe*'s Amos Kendall edited by his son-in-law, William Stickney, *Autobiography of Amos Kendall* (New York: Lee, Shepard and Dillingham, 1872); *New York Tribune*'s Horace Greeley and his autobiography, *Recollections of a Busy Life* (New York: J. B. Ford, 1868); *New York Times*'s Henry J. Raymond by staff member Augustus Maverick, *Henry J. Raymond and the New York Press, for Thirty Years: Progress of American Journalism from 1840 to 1870* (Hartford, Conn.: A. S. Hale, 1870); and *New York Herald*'s James Gordon Bennett emphasized over other editors by managing editor Frederic Hudson in his journalism history, *Journalism in the United States, from 1690 to 1872* (New York: Harper and Brothers, 1873).

2. Alfred McClung Lee, *The Daily Newspaper in America: The Evolution of a Social Instrument* (New York: Macmillan, 1937), 746, relying on U.S. Post Office Department data, and U.S. Bureau of the Census, *Historical Statistics of the United States, Colonial Times to 1970*, 2 parts (Washington, D.C.: Government Printing Office, 1975), 2: 731, 805.

3. F. Lawrence Babcock, *Spanning the Atlantic* (New York: Knopf, 1931), 50–51, and Carl H. Scheele, *A Short History of the Mail Service* (Washington, D.C.: Smithsonian Institution, 1970), 102.

4. Robert Luther Thompson, *Wiring a Continent: The History of the Telegraph Industry in the United States, 1832–1866* (Princeton, N.J.: Princeton University Press, 1947), 240 and facing map, relying on "Telegraphs," *Report of the Superintendent of the Census*, December 1, 1852, 106–7, and Charles B. Barr, comp., *Telegraph Stations in the United States, Canada and Nova Scotia, 1853* (Washington, D.C.: Library of Congress).

5. Frank Luther Mott, *American Journalism, A History: 1690–1960* (New York: Macmillan, 1962), 202–4, 315–16.

6. Maverick, *Raymond*, 89–90.

7. Hudson, *Journalism*, 536–37.

8. The post-Civil War "commercialization" of journalism is described by Gerald J. Baldasty in his *The Commercialization of the News in the Nineteenth Century* (Madison: University of Wisconsin Press, 1992).

9. A term used by Frank Luther Mott to describe American newspapering between 1801 and 1833. Mott, *Journalism*, 167.

10. Political and economic power was the payoff for an editor who had backed a winning candidate for public office. To have entrée to a new administration's inner circle, to have a public official's ear on policy question—even better, to be that official's "organ," his voice in print—was prestigious, elevating. But at least as rewarding for most editors was

to receive the government contract as the official reporter and printer of legislative proceedings or to print local court decisions, the administration's legal notices, or even the bureaucratic forms. For an especially well documented study of editors' political spoils, see Culver H. Smith, *The Press, Politics, and Patronage: The American Government's Use of Newspapers, 1789–1875* (Athens: University of Georgia Press, 1977).

11. Isaiah Thomas, *The History of Printing in America, with a Biography of Printers*, 2nd ed., 2 parts (1810; Albany, N.Y.: Joel Munsell, 1874; reprint ed., New York: Burt Franklin, n.d.), 2: 296–305. By the author's tabulation, there were 158 anti-Federalist Republican papers and 159 Federalist papers at the beginning of 1810, with twenty more calling themselves "neutral" and twenty-nine showing no political alliance.

12. Alexis de Tocqueville, *Democracy in America*, edited by Phillips Bradley, 2 vols. (1835, 1840; reprint ed. of Henry Reeve text, New York: Knopf, 1945), 1: 186–87.

13. The total of fourteen dailies is for 1850 and included nine morning and five evening papers in New York City. Eight of these dailies published Sunday editions. The dailies had a combined daily cirulation of 153,621 in 1850. One copy of a newspaper was sold for every four and one-half residents in the city, which had a total population of 696,115. Lee, *Daily*, 731, relying on W[illiam] T[urner] Coggeshall's *The Newspaper Record, Containing a Complete List of Newspapers and Periodicals in the United States, Canada, and Great Britain* . . . (Philadelphia: Lay and Brother, 1856).

14. The leading New York City penny papers in 1850 were the *Sun*, founded in 1833 by Benjamin Day and run after 1850 by brothers Moses S. and Alfred E. Beach, Democratic editorially and aiming police and court news for laborers and craftsmen with an 1850 daily circulation of 55,000; the *Herald*, founded in 1835 by James Gordon Bennett, moderately Democratic editorially and covering a broad spectrum of news useful to rising young white-collar office workers with an 1850 daily circulation of 32,640; and the *Tribune*, founded in 1841 by Horace Greeley, featuring strong Whig-later-Republican editorials and diverse essays examining alternative political and social theories with an 1850 daily circulation of 19,480. Circulations are reported in J[oseph] C[amp] G[riffith] Kennedy, *Catalogue of the Newspapers and Periodicals Published in the United States, Showing the Town and County in Which the Same Are Published, How Often Issued, Their Character, and Circulation* (New York: John Livingston, 1852), 29.

15. The leading New York City party papers in 1850 were the *Courier and Enquirer*, a strong Whig-later-Republican voice, merged by James Watson Webb in 1829, with an 1850 daily circulation of 5,200, and the *Express*, founded by brothers James and Erastus Brooks in 1836 and providing a political voice in turn to the Whigs, the Know-Nothings, and the Democrats with an 1850 daily circulation of 10,700. Circulations here are in Kennedy, *Catalogue*, 29.

16. Among several in New York City, the leading mercantile paper in

1850 was the *Journal of Commerce*, founded in 1827 and operated by Gerard Hallock, his partner, David Hale, having died in 1849. Editorially Democratic and proslavery, the paper reported its business news without bias, just as the demanding business community wanted it, with an 1850 daily circulation of 4,800. The circulation here is in Kennedy, *Catalogue*, 29.

17. Census, *Historical*, 1: 8, 2: 810.

18. The street prices of Chicago dailies are not discussed in the literature, and although both the *Times* and *Tribune* quote subscription prices for periods ranging from one week to one year on their front pages, neither shows a per-copy price.

19. "The Dead/The Living" [*Chicago Tribune* clipping from 1947], formerly available at the Chicago Public Library; Don E. Fehrenbacher, *Chicago Giant: A Biography of "Long John" Wentworth* (Madison, Wis.: The American History Research Center, 1957), 53, 73; Lloyd Wendt, *Chicago Tribune: The Rise of a Great American Newspaper* (Chicago: Rand McNally, 1979), 30, 33.

20. Fehrenbacher, *Giant*, 19–20, 189; Emmett Dedmon, *Fabulous Chicago* (New York: Random House, 1953), 26; Willis J. Abbot, "Chicago Newspapers and Their Makers," *Review of Reviews* (N.Y.) 11 (June 1895): 651; and Bessie Louise Pierce, *A History of Chicago*, 3 vols. (New York: Knopf, 1937, 1940, 1957; reprint ed. Chicago: University of Chicago Press, 1975), 2: 413.

21. Fehrenbacher, *Giant*, 188.

22. Wendt, *Tribune*, 23–24.

23. Pierce, *Chicago*, 413.

24. Quoted in Wendt, *Tribune*, 24.

25. Quoted in Wendt, *Tribune*, 64.

26. To be precise, the *Times* began life as the nonpartisan *Chicago Courant*, owned by William D. Wilson and A. C. Cameron and first issued in November of 1853. In June of 1854, Douglas supporters Isaac Cook, Daniel Cameron, and J. W. Patterson purchased the paper and changed the name to the *Times*. Pierce, Chicago, 2: 414, and Justin E. Walsh, *To Print the News and Raise Hell! A Biography of Wilbur F. Storey* (Chapel Hill: University of North Carolina Press, 1968), 150.

27. Robin L. Einhorn, *Property Rules: Political Economy in Chicago, 1833–1872* (Chicago: University of Chicago Press, 1991), 158–59.

28. Walsh, *Storey*, 5, 48–49; Fehrenbacher, *Giant*, 130–31; and Wendt, *Tribune*, 23, 35–36.

29. J. D. B. DeBow, Census Office, U.S. Department of Interior, *Statistical View of the United States . . . Being a Compendium of the Seventh Census* (Washington, D.C.: A. O. P. Nicholson Public Printer, 1854), 372, and Joseph C. G. Kennedy, Census Office, U.S. Department of Interior, *Population of the United States in 1860* (Washington, D.C.: Government Printing Office, 1864), xxxii.

30. Lee, *Daily*, 613–15.

31. Wendt, *Tribune*, 64.

32. DeBow, *Seventh Census*, 347, and Kennedy, *Population . . . 1860*, xxxi.

33. Walsh, *Storey*, 162.

34. Franc B. Wilkie, *Personal Reminiscences of Thirty-five Years of Journalism* (Chicago: F. J. Schulte, 1891), 93, 103–4, 107, 108–10.

35. Walsh, *Storey*, 162, 226.

36. Portions of this sketch of nineteenth-century journalists rely on Fred Fedler's *Lessons from the Past: Journalists' Lives and Work, 1850–1950* (Prospect Heights, Ill.: Waveland Press, 2000), esp. 11–36, 137–53.

37. Richard A. Schwarzlose, *The Nation's Newsbrokers*, 2 vols. (Evanston, Ill.: Northwestern University Press, 1989–90), 1: 136–46, 227–34.

38. Pierce, *Chicago*, 2: 160–61. An "em" is a measure of linear type based on the point size of the type being set. If a compositor is setting six-point type, an em equals six points. And if the compositor is setting fifteen-pica-wide newspaper columns (columns that are two-and-a-half inches wide), then (given that a pica equals twelve points) each line consist of 180 points or thirty ems. If the compositor's pay is based on thirty cents per thousand ems, he will have to set a little more than thirty-three lines of type to earn thirty cents.

39. Meyer Berger, *The Story of The New York Times, 1851–1951* (New York: Simon and Schuster, 1951), 5.

40. Arthur T. Turnbull and Russell N. Baird, *The Graphics of Communication: Typography-Layout-Design*, 2nd ed. (New York: Holt, Rinehart and Winston, 1968), 57–85, and this author's experience with typesetting. A composing stick is a four-sided metal box, one side adjustable to form the desired column width and the other two sides open to receive the type.

41. Maverick, *Raymond*, 158–59.

42. Elizabeth Faulkner Baker, *Printers and Technology: A History of the International Printing Pressmen and Assistants' Union* (New York: Columbia University Press, 1957), 51.

43. Pierce, *Chicago*, 2: 160, 162–64, and Walsh, Storey, 224.

44. James Moran, *Printing Presses: History and Development from the Fifteenth Century to Modern Times* (Berkeley: University of California Press, 1973), 105–10, 139.

45. Moran, *Presses*, 185–87, and Frank E. Comparato, *Chronicles of Genius and Folly: R. Hoe & Company and the Printing Press as a Service to Democracy* (Culver City, Calif.: Labyrinthos, 1979), 261–303.

46. Moran, *Presses*, 190–92.

47. Wendt, *Tribune*, 30, 32.

48. Pierce, *Chicago*, 2: 414, and Wendt, *Tribune*, 153, 197. The *Tribune* in 1861 proudly inserted a line etching of a four-cylinder type-revolver being worked by four pressmen in its nameplate between *Chicago* and *Tribune*.

49. Walsh, *Storey*, 162.

50. "How The Times looked when one day old," Berger, *Story*, opposite 4.

51. Author's collection of mid-nineteenth-century newspapers, and newspaper files at the Northwestern University Library, Evanston, Ill., and the Chicago Public Library.

52. Hudson, *Journalism*, 258.

53. Kathleen L. Endres, "Civil War Press (North)," *History of the Mass Media in the United States: An Encyclopedia*, ed. by Margaret A. Blanchard (Chicago: Fitzroy Dearborn Publishers, 1998), 141.

54. J. Cutler Andrews, *The North Reports the Civil War* (Pittsburgh: University of Pittsburgh Press, 1955), 751–59, and *The South Reports the Civil War* (Princeton, N. J.: Princeton University Press, 1970), 548–51.

55. Mott, *Journalism*, 329.

56. *Democrat, Herald, Illinois Staats-Zeitung, Journal, Post, Times, Tribune,* and *Truth*. "Dead/Living."

57. *Cincinnati Gazette*, July 5, 1863, reprinted in part in Louis L. Snyder and Richard B. Morris, *A Treasury of Great Reporting* (New York: Simon and Schuster, 1949), 145–46.

58. Andrews, *North*, 644.

59. Associated Press (Illinois), *Annual Report* (1896), 156.

60. William Henry Smith, "Appendix," Western Associated Press, *Proceedings* (1876), 25–82.

61. "New York Associated Press Agreement with Chicago Papers," printed document dated Cleveland, March 25, 1865, William Henry Smith Papers, Indiana Historical Society, Indianapolis.

62. Walsh, *Storey*, 146.

63. Walsh, *Storey*, 149.

64. Wilkie, *Reminiscences*, 100.

65. Pierce, *Chicago*, 2: 415.

66. Walsh, *Storey*, 160, and Pierce, *Chicago*, 2: 415.

67. Walsh, *Storey*, 182–83.

68. Pierce, *Chicago*, 2: 416.

69. Theodore J. Karamanski, *Rally 'Round the Flag: Chicago and the Civil War* (Chicago: Nelson-Hall, 1993), 193.

70. Pierce, *Chicago*, 2: 416.

71. Walsh, *Storey*, 4.

72. Michael Schudson, *Discovering the News: A Social History of American Newspapers* (New York: Basic Books, 1978), 67.

73. Mott, *Journalism*, 388.

74. Wilkie, *Reminiscences*, 130–31.

75. Walsh, *Storey*, 201-2.

76. Walsh, *Storey*, 216, quoting the *Chicago Times* for August 7, 1865.

77. Karamanski, *Rally*, 190.

78. Hazel Dicken-Garcia, *Journalistic Standards in Nineteenth-Century America* (Madison: University of Wisconsin Press, 1989), 184–85.

79. Baldasty, *Commercialization*, 67, 73. The quote is from an 1899 issue of the *Profitable Advertiser*, a Boston trade journal.

80. Hudson, *Journalism*, 258.

Introduction

IN 1994, when I was asked to write a biographical essay on John M. Wing for the *Dictionary of Literary Biography: American Book Collectors and Bibliographers* (vol. 187), I thought to myself, "piece of cake." After twenty-odd years as a user of books and manuscripts in the Wing Foundation at the Newberry Library, Chicago, I had heard most of the stories about Wing that circulated among the staff: he was a nineteenth-century Chicago publisher who made a bundle from trade publications and retired at the age of forty-four. He spent his retirement traveling, purchasing books and prints to illustrate them, and was, according to an inscription in one of these lavishly decorated volumes, "a batchelor by the grace of God." When he died, he left the Newberry nearly a quarter of a million dollars and his personal library, with the stipulation that the interest from this endowment be used to create a collection on the history of Western printing from its beginnings in fifteenth-century Europe and to pay the salary of a custodian for the collection.

The Wing Foundation was the first American public collection devoted to the history of printing and is one of the best collections on all aspects of printing, containing both primary and secondary materials on typography, printing presses, printers, graphic designers, papermaking, bookbinding, and book illustration. Its collection of printed calligraphy and penmanship manuals is without peer in the world. But there really did not seem to be much to write about Wing as a collector (practically all the books in the Wing Foundation were acquired from the endowment and not from his personal library), let alone as an individual, and I even wondered whether I could come up with the required five thousand words. That was until I started my research on him.

The first thing I did was to check with Paul F. Gehl, Custodian of the Wing Foundation, about any available biographical or autobiographical material. Paul had plenty to show me—library reports, a master's thesis on the Wing Foundation, Wing's genealogical writings, scrapbooks, the famous "extra-illustrated" books, and his last will and testament. Then Paul casually asked if I had ever looked at Wing's diaries. Diaries? Of course not, he mused, since they had never been catalogued. He got them from the vault, and I began reading—with some difficulty—the juvenilia of John Mansir Wing.

I got through the earliest diaries quickly, as the barely fourteen-year-old Wing recorded only such things as the weather, visitors, and visits to friends and relatives in upstate, rural New York. Not until I reached those covering his apprenticeship in a newspaper print shop and his first job as a country schoolteacher did the diaries really grab my attention. In these volumes, a picture emerges of not only his teen years but also some of the events that would shape his life.

Although his formal education was scant by today's standards—ending by the time he was sixteen—it was rigorous. Besides mathematics, algebra, and grammar, Wing also studied Latin and rhetoric at the Pulaski Academy, in upstate New York, where he received most of his schooling. He belonged to an extracurricular group that met once a week to read aloud original essays, thereby honing both writing and oratorical skills. Wing continued both his reading and writing after leaving school and always tried to improve himself intellectually as much as possible in what he considered rustic circumstances.

A voracious reader, Wing often recorded his favorite books in his early diaries—Shakespeare's plays, the poetry of Shelley and Byron (all of *Don Juan*), the novels of Benjamin Disraeli, *The Pickwick Papers*, and other works, mostly by British authors. Some of the American authors he read are little known today, but one who was quite popular in her day may have colored Wing's approach to life more than any Englishman he read. On October 1, 1859, he recorded finishing Mrs. Southworth's *Hid-*

den Hand, which had been serialized in the *New York Ledger* that year. Emma Southworth (1819–99) wrote sixty-seven novels (some of which sold in the hundreds of thousands) and is credited with introducing "two new character types to American fiction: the self-made man and the independent woman" (*Merriam-Webster Encylopedia of Literature,* 1995). It was shortly after reading Southworth that Wing adopted *Labor Omnia Vincit* as his personal motto.

Although he never says so, I suspect the early attraction to some of these authors reflected the tastes of teachers at the Pulaski Academy, from whom he borrowed books, as much as his own teenage predisposition. In any case, this Anglophilia took, and a substantial number of the four thousand–plus books he left to the Newberry Library are by or about British subjects. He collected little significant American literature—no Emerson, no Melville, no Twain, no Whitman, to mention only a few of his literary contemporaries.

Wing loved school and hated the times he spent as what he called a "rusticus" on the family tenant farm near Pulaski. But to stay in school he had to work to pay his tuition, and he knew he was not cut out to be a farmer. So in 1860 he took a job for three months as a printer's devil at the *Pulaski Democrat.* It was in this local newspaper that his first published piece appeared, a poem called "The Man Within," and although he was less than happy with his work as an apprentice, he was thrilled to see his words in print.

In the fall of 1860, after lying about his age, Wing got his teacher's certificate and that winter obtained work at a country school. As in the printing office, Wing loathed this job, and the local school board was equally displeased with his teaching. After three months, his contract was not renewed. Since no other teaching jobs were forthcoming near his home, Wing moved to Oswego, New York, where he found work on a local paper "collecting the telegraph," that is, copying the daily reports that kept the most remote newspapers abreast of national news. This job began in late March 1861, only a few weeks before the outbreak of the Civil War. Having little experience in gathering or reporting the news, Wing was abruptly let go by the *Oswego Times* the day after the war began. He soon found another job much more to his liking, clerking in a bookstore, which gave him unlimited access to books. He even had a bookplate printed for his burgeoning library at that time.

In the late summer of 1861, Wing returned to school briefly but could not afford the tuition. Another short stint at teaching occurred early in 1862, and shortly after his eighteenth birthday, Wing began working as an apprentice typesetter and printer on the *Black River Herald* in Boonville, New York. He would never return to school as either pupil or teacher.

He was a quick learner and within a few months became a prodigious typesetter. He published both his prose and poetry in the *Pulaski Democrat* and the *Black River Herald* under the nom de plume of *Labor Omnia Vincit* (or *LOV*), words that expressed his Yankee (and Emma Southworth's) belief that hard work would bring rewards and success.

During the war, his published writings increased, as he wrote poems for other local newspapers, then news articles and editorials, and he dutifully recorded their titles in his diaries. This habit, along with keeping scrapbooks of his published writings, appears in his Chicago diaries. His newspaper scrapbooks probably perished in the great Chicago fire of 1871, but the careful listing of his newspaper articles in the diaries has made it possible to locate his news writings for the *Chicago Times* and the *Republican*, given here in an appendix.

Wing left the *Black River Herald* at the end of the year and took a typesetting job on the *Roman Citizen* in nearby Rome, New York, where he became a journeyman printer within a year. In January 1864, Wing moved again, this time to Utica, New York, and to a job as a proofreader and then reporter on the *Utica Herald*. Despite his sometimes eighteen-hour days, Wing continued to write for several upstate papers. Having learned all parts of the newspaper business, from typesetting to operating a press to proofreading to reporting, he even considered buying a small rural newspaper in December 1864. Instead, he took his last New York job in Oswego.

Labor did, indeed, *omnia vincit*, and Wing was hired as a reporter on the *Oswego Commercial Advertiser* in January 1865.

Ironically, Wing was fired from this job a few weeks after the end of the Civil War, just as he had been fired in the same city from the *Times* at the beginning of the war. He had just turned twenty-one.

In many ways, the Civil War must have shaped Wing but not in an obvious fashion. The 1861–65 diaries are nearly completely devoid of war references, something I found puzzling at first. However, Wing was far removed from battle, had few friends fighting and only one close relative in the war (his stepbrother, whom he disliked), and was working for newspapers for most of this period. During the war, he had gathered news from telegraph reports, set type for articles about the conflict, proofread war copy, and wrote editorials on the war. So the diaries did not contain "news" of current military events, something that would have been redundant to his daily activities, but rather were about Wing's favorite subject, John M. Wing. But then are not all diaries the product of a certain amount of narcissism? The war affected Wing the way wars have always affected young men, in or out of service—it made him more aware of a larger world beyond his native Holmesville, and almost as soon as the war was over, he left the small towns of New York State to try his fortunes in the great West.

It is difficult to say how much a seemingly trivial factor played in Wing's decision to go West: as a reporter for the *Oswego Advertiser*, he had received a complimentary pass from the Northern Transportation Company, a steamship company whose ships plied the Great Lakes from New York state to Illinois. Such perks were not uncommon in the newspaper business of the time, often a reward (or more likely a bribe) for a mention of an individual or company in a "news" story. Wing was a master of such "puffs," and since he perpetually moaned about his poverty in all the diaries, a pass on a steamship line would have appeared as money in an empty pocket. So on May 30 he boarded a westbound steamship on Lake Ontario, even though he was no longer an employee of the *Advertiser*.

His steamer stopped at Cleveland and Detroit, and in both places Wing sought newspaper work without success. From Detroit he went to Ann Arbor to visit a friend, and failing to find

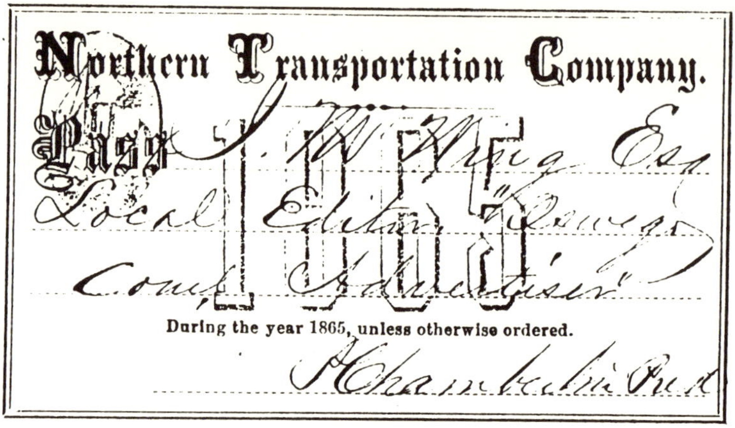
Northern Transportation Company.

Pass

During the year 1865, unless otherwise ordered.

Pass issued to "J. M. Wing, Esq. Local Editor 'Oswego Coml Advertiser' " by the Northern Transportation Company.

him, took the night train to Chicago. The diary entries transcribed here begin with his arrival in the city on June 4, a hot Sunday afternoon.

* * *

Postwar Chicago was certainly a rough-and-tumble town—or rather a city of nearly a quarter million—but as the diaries show, it was also a place of some culture. Wing's first newspaper assignment was to write a review of the Italian opera *Norma,* and throughout the diaries we find him often going to the theater. Chicago theaters not only presented some of the newest European musical works such as Giuseppe Verdi's 1862 opera *La forza del destino* and Charles Gounod's 1859 *Faust* to a large audience (Crosby's Opera House seated nearly as many people as does the present Lyric Opera House of Chicago), they also put on the latest British and American plays and featured the leading actors of the day. Wing's recurring visits to Col. Wood's Theatre and Museum were probably encouraged by a free pass he must have obtained as a reporter. (Such a pass can be assumed both by the frequency of his visits and the relatively rare mentions of visits to the city's other theaters.) He clearly enjoyed the theater, and on one occasion when he had fallen behind in his diary (7/28/65), he guesses at what he did that day and concludes (in the third person): "But judging from his habits it is fair to infer that he went to the theatre."

Chicago contained forty-five booksellers and stationers when Wing arrived, and he bought books from several of them. The variety of his purchases indicates that these shops were stocked with both new and antiquarian titles. Wing is annoyingly vague most of the time about what he buys, commenting more on the bargain he got than the name of the book, but sometimes it is possible to narrow down his purchases when he does give an author or title. His youthful preferences in books remained constant into his old age: British poetry and literature and Continental literature. Indeed, only one American author, Nathaniel Hawthorne, is mentioned in these diaries, but there is no indication that Wing ever read his *Twice-Told Tales*.

Other levels of postwar literacy in the city are indicated by the number of daily, weekly, and monthly publications produced in Chicago in 1865: seven daily newspapers (two in German) and some nineteen weekly papers that covered topics from music to religion to commerce to sports. Chicago magazine publications were predominantly professional in nature: the *American Law Manual* was a quarterly, and the *Chicago Medical Journal, The Peoples' Journal of Health,* and *Haines Legal Adviser* appeared monthly. These were but a few of the eleven journals produced in the city. And although it was true that Chicago lacked a general public library before the Great Fire of 1871, when Wing came to the city there were seven libraries and reading rooms available to its citizens and one library just for the employees of the Illinois Central Railroad.

Wing's infamous article on immigrant Irish shanty towns (see Appendix C) and its near disastrous results for the *Times* reveal something that is frequently overlooked in Chicago histories. Some five thousand Irish threatened to cancel their subscriptions and put the paper under. Now Irish immigrants (second only to the Germans in number in Chicago just before the war) totaled near twenty thousand in 1860. So with five thousand-plus *Times* subscribers, this population was not only a relatively literate group but also a significant political and economic force in the city by the end of the war.

* * *

Diaries have been compared to artists' sketchbooks. Both are usually first impressions spontaneously put down for future reference (or not) and lack many details that might be included in subsequent renderings. The Chicago diaries of John Wing fit this description. They abound in spelling errors, grammatical mistakes, and tortured syntax, all surprising for someone who often acted as an editor of the writing of others; but this is perfectly in keeping with the sketchy nature of the entries, sometimes written after an exhausting day, on the fly, or days or weeks after the events recorded. To maintain the immediacy of Wing's writing, I have presented a diplomatic transcription of his text, "complete, with all faults," as booksellers say. I have also decided to spare the reader the irritatingly pedantic use of *sic* every time an error appears: all "mistakes" within the entries are those of Wing. Occasionally I have inserted a word or expanded an abbreviation for the sake of clarity, always enclosing them in square brackets to distinguish them from Wing's writing. Since Wing knew standard proofreading marks (the same in the 1860s as they are now), I have not transcribed his single, double, or triple underscores but have presented these as italic, small capitals, and capitals, respectively. As with his spelling, he was not consistent in their use either, sometimes giving the names of newspapers in italic, sometimes in small capitals.

In editing the diaries, I have tried to clarify those words, idioms, places, people, and events that might be unfamiliar to a modern reader, as well as give some sense of what Wing experienced in the city by adding notes immediately after an entry when they seem necessary. Sources for these notes are not indicated in the text lest the whole thing turn into a set of nesting Russian dolls, with notes within notes. In most cases, the source of a note can be determined from the references at the end of this book. Naturally, Wing's newspaper articles and pamphlets give information that other publications do not, and a list of these is provided in appendix B. A major source of information about the local people Wing met comes from contemporary Chicago city directories, which give not only the addresses of those listed but also their occupations. For the famous people he mentioned or wrote about, I relied on the *Dictionary of American Biography*. The standard histories of Chicago also proved valuable in sorting out many of the people and events Wing encountered.

The diaries themselves present many problems to an editor, not the least of which is Wing's handwriting (see the illustration facing page 3). For example, *o* looks like *a* and vice versa, *i* and *e* are sometimes indistinguishable, *u, v* and *n* are triplets, and *d* frequently looks like *l, cl,* or *ch* (which in one early diary led to a momentary misreading of *direful* as *cheerful*). Eventually, I grew accustomed to most of these idiosyncrasies, but there were still a few times when I was completely stumped by his scrawl, and his idiosyncratic syntax offered no help whatsoever. In those instances, I have indicated this in the note to that diary entry.

Wing was inconsistent about spelling names, usually giving a phonetic spelling first and a more correct spelling later, after he had either been told or had seen (sometimes on a calling card) the right spelling. But even with people he had known for years, he sometimes spelled their names erratically. I have tried to catch those instances in which Wing has misspelled a personal name or used a nickname for a friend and identify the individual in a note following the diary entry as he or she appears elsewhere in these and other diaries or published sources.

* * *

Paul Gehl points out in his foreword that these diaries are not the richest source for pre-fire Chicago history. Indeed, outside of identifying the author of more than one hundred newspaper articles and the detailed accounts of preparing a nineteenth-century pamphlet for publication, the diaries do not add that much to our historical knowledge. They really are mostly about Jack Wing, and their value lies more in the realm of biography. But even when one regards the text as biographical material, I would caution the reader to notice what is *not* there, as well as what is. For instance, on Christmas day 1865 the only present Wing recorded receiving was a box of cigars from Billy Bolshaw. As I note, Bolshaw was proprietor of the

Matteson House Saloon and Billiard Room, a few doors east of Col. Wood's Theatre, so it seems plausible that Wing probably "dropped in for a moment" at Bolshaw's as frequently as he did at the Colonel's. How else to explain this generous gift? Although Bolshaw is mentioned only once more in the diaries, he took an ad in Wing's stockyard pamphlet, suggesting a closeness not apparent from reading the diaries. This led me to think further about Wing's drinking habits. Rarely did he mention his drinking in Chicago, something I found curious in a city where saloons abounded. The entry for August 31, 1865, mentions "a drunken party on the steamer Planet" and the ensuing commotion, but Wing appears almost as an innocent bystander, being attacked later on a streetcar by rowdy Board of Trade members. Could it be that he had become ashamed of his tippling or thought recording such activities was unworthy of his diary? Only a year before, he had written about several drunken sprees he went on in upstate New York. It should be recalled that temperance was a major issue in nineteenth-century America, and drinking hard liquor carried a social stigma in some circles. Genteel drinks with General Grant or the brothers at Notre Dame was one thing; hitting the saloons was quite another. In any case, always the rebel, Wing later started an antitemperance trade journal, *The Western Brewer*.

Much will be made over Wing's intimate encounters with young men, yet unlike his drinking, he wrote freely about these episodes, sometimes in a most romantic way. Modern scholarship has revealed such intimacies between men (and between women) were neither uncommon nor socially unacceptable throughout the nineteenth century. The youthful diaries and letters of such prominent Americans as Daniel Webster and Ralph Waldo Emerson show Wing was not alone in his late adolescent attachments to members of his own sex. And who can forget this striking American literary instance of two men sharing a bed? "Upon waking next morning about daylight, I found Queequeg's arm thrown over me in the most loving and affectionate manner. You had almost thought I had been his wife." Herman Melville published this in *Moby-Dick* in 1851, less than a decade before Wing began keeping his diaries.

From the earlier diaries, it is clear that Wing found sharing a bed with someone he knew a way of gaining more of a social than a physical closeness, of bonding with another, if you will. A homoerotic aspect cannot totally be discounted, especially in those instances in which Wing takes a complete stranger into his bed. Stranger or friend, he always romanticized his bedmate. With the shifty Tommy Phelan, it was not only his military service and uniform but also the time he spent as a prisoner of war in Andersonville that no doubt appealed to Wing. One can positively see Wing cringe when Phelan reappears "in a horrible old suit of citizens clothes," looking just like an average man. This now sartorially-challenged youth soon disappears from the diary and Wing's thoughts.

In June 1864, Wing was invited to become a member of a nonacademic fraternity, Upsilon Beta (referred to as YB in the diaries). Like many adolescent, all-male organizations, his fraternity could be viewed as a homoerotic society, but for Jack it became a rich source of friendships. The YBs had chapters scattered around New York state, with members as far west as St. Louis, and Jack often took weekend trips to visit members while living in Utica and Oswego. He became an officer, returning to New York from Chicago to attend fraternity conventions, and his diaries frequently mentioned correspondence to and from his fellow YBs. In fact, the side trip from Detroit to Ann Arbor that eventually led to his arrival in Chicago was to visit a fraternity brother. But his diaries also include rare amorous encounters with women, and only a year before joining the YB fraternity, Wing had an intense romance with a young girl.

While working in Rome, New York, Wing was introduced to "Miss Fan Churchill, a gay young lady of 16 summers," as he describes her in his diary (6/30/63). The attraction was mutual, surprising the nineteen-year-old Wing: "Fan is in love with me, dear little fire-fly, and I am about as much in love myself—though it is the first time my feelings were ever disturbed by a female" (7/2/63). Wing does not write much about their relationship other than to indicate that Fan was the aggressor in the affair, giving him gifts and allowing him to kiss her and caress her in private. Their romance did not survive the fall, however.

By mid-November, Fan was writing Wing for the return of the jewelry and other gifts she had given him. Still, he writes of her occasionally in his Chicago diaries as "'the only girl I ever loved' and the only one I fear that will ever love me" (10/27/65).

* * *

There are few records of Wing's life after the diaries: new editions of his pamphlet on the lake tunnel were printed in Chicago in 1867 and 1868, indicating he was still in the city at least part of those years. In March 1868, he went to Europe for five months as overseas correspondent for the *Boston Journal* and as traveling companion to the publisher's son. Besides his articles on Europe printed in the *Journal,* his entertaining letters to his sister Anna also survive. His hopes for a job in Boston were dashed with the untimely death of the *Journal*'s publisher, and sometime in 1869 Wing returned to Chicago, where he established his own publishing house, J. M. Wing and Company, Publishers. The first publication he issued was a monthly illustrated magazine on Chicago real estate, *The Land Owner.* After the fire, he published short books of Chicago boosterism such as *Rebuilt Chicago.* He also brought his parents and sister to live with him in his house on Congress Avenue. In 1876 Wing added *The Western Brewer,* another trade journal, to his regular publications, and issued an annual, *Wing's Brewers' Hand-Book of the United States and Canada* in 1877. Despite their profitability—and Wing's publishing ventures were profitable, *The Land Owner* making him as much as $35,000 a year, tax-free—he ceased publication of *The Land Owner* in 1877, the annual in 1884, and *The Western Brewer* in 1887; and in 1888 he retired at the age of forty-four. Although there are no surviving records to prove it, he probably had investments in property or stocks, since when he died twenty-nine years later his estate was worth around a quarter of a million dollars.

His life after retirement was not particularly lavish. He indulged himself in trips to Europe and the east coast, continued to acquire books, and bought many thousands of prints for his pastime of extra-illustrating books. Extra-illustrating had been invented in eighteenth-century England and became a hobby for some book collectors who did not consider inserting prints (and later, photographs) into a text a desecration. Wing followed the guidelines laid down in the 1881 *Monograph on Privately-Illustrated Books* by Daniel M. Tredwell, who warned against destroying books of great value by adding cheap illustrations to them. Wing sometimes did the exact opposite, illustrating cheap books with some uncommon and occasionally significant seventeenth-century engravings.

One of the most curious aspects of Wing's later life in Chicago is a total absence of participation in any of the city's cultural institutions after his retirement. Chicago history seems to have reciprocated this postretirement disinterest, for despite his place in Chicago publishing and philanthropy, Wing's name is conspicuously absent from histories of the city's movers and shakers, even though no serious history of Chicago can be written without reference to many of his publications, especially *The Land Owner*. He was never a member of the Caxton Club, the Arts Club, the Masons, nor any other social organization. Perhaps, like Groucho Marx, he did not want to belong to any club that would have him as a member. The only local institution Wing showed an early interest in was the Newberry Library. In one of his scrapbooks preserved at the library are several clippings on its construction. Wing, however, was not antisocial, as the few surviving letters from him to friends in Chicago and New York indicate.

In 1900 Wing published a rather fanciful autobiography in his family's genealogical journal *The Owl*, where he indicated he planned to establish the "John M. Wing Foundation at the Newberry Library." His article makes no mention of the nature of his endowment and might have come as a surprise to the library, since there is no record of any contact with the Newberry before 1912. (An 1899 letter to him from the Newberry's Librarian, E. W. Blatchford, survives but has nothing to do with Wing's intentions for the institution.) In 1913 Wing deposited his books in the Newberry Library and was given his own room, where the books were stored and where he acted as his own docent for the collection, showing them to any interested visitor. It was also in this year that he wrote his first will relating to the Newberry Library (revised in 1914 and 1915), specifying the establishment of a foundation for the creation of a collection on the history of western printing and providing for the salary of a curator. He continued to extra-illustrate his books in the library, and they were bound by the Newberry's bookbinder. He also sold his house in 1913 and lived in hotels the remaining years of his life.

On the first Friday in March 1917, Wing caught a chill in the library and at 1:30 A.M. the following Monday, he died of pneumonia in his room at the Auditorium Hotel.

From an early age, Wing aspired to be a writer, first of poetry, then essays, editorials, and finally journalism. But in reading his diaries, I think he may have missed one form of writing with which he had great skill—the short story. Throughout the Chicago diaries are perfect miniature tales of his life. Somehow Jack made the ordinary seem extraordinary and, in doing so, I hope, still gives the reader pleasure.

* * *

When I came to these diaries, I was not overly familiar with nineteenth-century American history, and my awareness of Chicago history was pretty much what I had gained in the Chicago public-school system. So as I worked on the Wing diaries, I found I had much to discover about the city and the period. In this I was helped by many people whom I thank here. No one can really write about Chicago without the help of the staff of the Chicago Historical Society Library. Their knowledgable assistance led me to the identification and location of such places as Camp Fry and the Soldier's Rest, and among the library's resources I discovered more about 1860 Chicago grain elevators than I could ever have imagined. It was also in the Chicago Historical Society Library that I found a map with street numbers that made it possible for me to give more precise locations of some of the places Wing mentions in his diaries. Annette Fern, now research and reference librarian of the Harvard Theatre Collection and long-time opera companion when she lived in Chicago, enlightened me on nineteenth-century opera and theater in Chicago and steered me to several important sources. Alice Schreyer, curator of special collections at the University of Chicago and fellow Caxtonian, alerted me to the Napier Wilt *Drama Performance Index*, truly a gold mine on early Chicago theater. The staff at the Newberry Library in special collections, the general reading room, and the reference desk are practically family members and have always been ready to help me with some of the problems I faced in transcribing and annotating these diaries.

Since I have worked in publishing for more than three decades, I know that no book is possible without the assistance of many people. Without Paul Gehl, these diaries would have never seen the light of day. Paul has encouraged and enlightened me from the very beginning, and it was he who first suggested the diaries be published. The Caxton Club publications committee—Susan Rossen (chair), Bruce Beck (honorary chair), Matt Doherty, Paul Gehl, Celia Hilliard, Wendy Husser, and Frank Piehl—read an early draft of the diaries and accepted them for publication under their distinguished imprint. Susan Rossen acted as a facilitator, seeking out a university publisher and putting me in touch with my first editor and fellow Caxtonian, Kathleen Kuiper. Thanks to Kathleen's editorial queries, I have added many annotations that I hope will make the diaries clearer and, thanks to her blue pencil, will make sense. Wayne Larsen, my copy editor at Southern Illinois University Press, has further refined my prose, so whatever sylistic infelicities remain are my responsibilities. (I fear much of my sympathy for Jack Wing comes from a shared love of tortured syntax!) Richard Schwarzlose, professor at the Medill School of Journalism, Northwestern University, came to the project as an expert on the history of journalism, and his essay helps us all understand the state of midcentury journalism in Chicago. Finally, I am grateful to Southern Illinois University Press for making this the first copublished Caxton Club title in the club's 107-year history. John M. Wing would most likely approve of this effort to extend the reach of his observations as far and as wide as possible.

Robert Williams

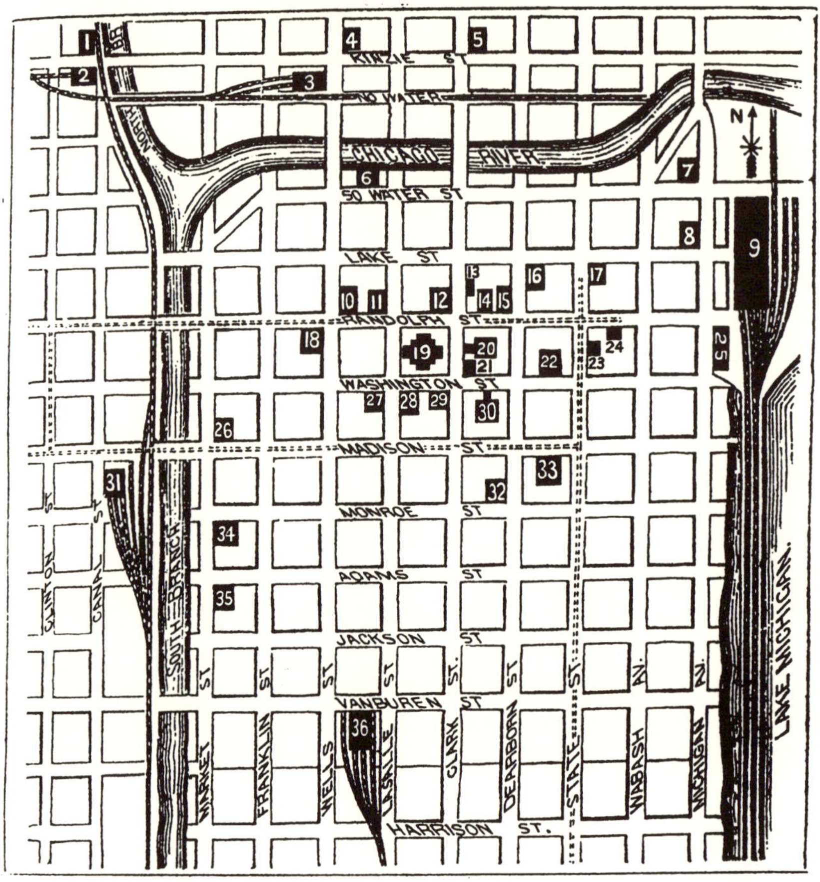

Jack Wing's Chicago: Map from *Edwards' Annual Directory, 1866–1867.*

1 Northwestern Railroad Passenger and Freight Depot

2 Milwaukee Railroad Passenger and Freight Depot

3 Galena Division Passenger Depot of the Northwestern Railroad

4 Historical Society and Library

5 The Revere House

6 [The old Board of Trade Building]

7 The Richmond House

8 The Adams House

9 The Great Union Passenger Depot of the Illinois, Michigan Central, and the Chicago, Burlington and Quincy Railroads

10 The Briggs House

11 Metropolitan Hall. Eastman's; Northwestern Business College

12 The Sherman House

13 [*Chicago Tribune* Office]

14 Col. Wood's Theatre and Museum

15 The Matteson House

16 The Tremont House

17 [City Hotel]

18 The Metropolitan Hotel

19 The Court House [City Hall]

20 [Bryan Hall]

21 Larmon Block; Bryant & Stratton's Chicago Business College

22 Crosby's Opera House

23 The City Railway

24 [City Omnibus Office]

25 [Dearborn Park]

26 The Garden City Hotel

27 Police Headquarters

28 The Board of Trade Building

29 Smith & Nixon's Concert Hall

30 The Academy of Music

31 West Side Union Depot of the Chicago and St. Louis Railroad, and the Pittsburgh and Fort Wayne Railroad

32 The Post Office, Custom House and Revenue Collector's Office

33 McVicker's Theatre

34 City Gas and Coke Works (Dickey's Building)

35 The Armory, Police Justices' Court and Court of Reform School

36 Rock Island Railroad, and the Michigan Southern and Lake Shore Railroad Depot

Dotted lines: Horse Railway and Omnibus routes (street cars)

Names in square brackets are not given on the 1866–67 map of the downtown area, nor are the east-west alleys between the blocks shown. This map, which was used for several years without revision, also omits the State Street bridge over the Chicago River that was present in Wing's time.

The Chicago Diaries of

JOHN M. WING

1865–1866

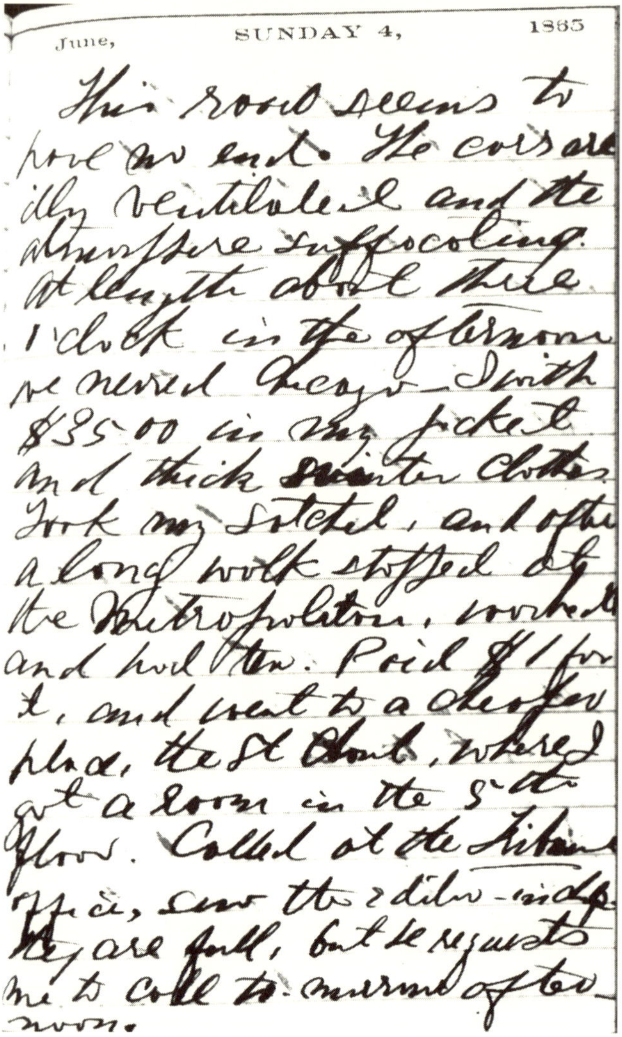
June, SUNDAY 4, 1865

This road seems to
have no end. The cars are
illy ventilated and the
atmosphere suffocating.
At length about three
o'clock in the afternoon
we reached Chicago—I with
$35.00 in my pocket
and thick winter clothes.
Took my satchel, and after
a long walk stopped at
the Metropolitan, washed
and had tea. Paid $1 for
it, and went to a cheaper
place, the St [illegible], where I
got a room in the 5th
floor. Called at the Tribune
office, saw the editor-in-chief.
They are full, but he requests
me to call to-morrow after-
noon.

"This road seems to have no end." Jack Wing arrives in Chicago Sunday afternoon, June 4, 1865. Reproduced actual size.

1865 Diary: June–December

Sunday 4 This road seems to have no end. The cars are illy ventilated and the atmosphere suffocating. At length, about three o'clock in the afternoon, we neared Chicago—I with $35.00 in my jacket and thick winter clothes. Took my satchel, and after a long walk stopped at the Metropolitan, washed and had tea. Paid $1 for it, and went to a cheaper place, the St. Cloud, where I got a room in the 5th floor. Called at the *Tribune* office, saw the editor-in chief, they are full, but he requests me to call to-morrow afternoon.

Metropolitan: hotel on the southwest corner of Randolph and Wells streets. **St. Cloud:** hotel on the west side of Franklin Street, between Washington and Madison streets.

Monday 5 Slept rather late, then took my first Chicago breakfast, and a poor one it was. The heat is intense, and I am sweltering beneath my thick garments. Called at the *Journal* office, but the expected verdict was "all full." Went to the Republican office with a gloomy mind, and there met the same response. Went to the Tribune office and the Chief Local [editor] said that he would set me at work writing notices of the Opera and of paintings. O! that I was adequate now.

heat: The high this day in downtown Chicago was 89 degrees. ***Journal* . . . Republican:** Chicago newspapers. The first issue of the *Republican* had just appeared on May 30th of this year. **Tribune:** on the east side of Clark between Randolph and Lake streets.

Tuesday 6 At the Tribune office and was directed to do some court reporting, which I got through with quite satisfactorily. Then was given a ticket and told to go to the Opera and write it up. ¶Went to the Italian Opera at the great new opera House—the finest in the country. The opera was "Norma," paid the closest attention to the plot, and the singing, but never saw an opera of the kind before, and was not able to judge at all. Wrote out a report of it, and then saw it criticised and cut down, but the most of it printed.

reporting: W generally uses this term to refer to rewriting reports and news stories as opposed to actually covering a news story. See 6/8/65. W kept a scrapbook of his articles and had done court reporting and covered theatrical and musical events while working for various newspapers in upstate New York. He must have shown these articles to the Chicago editors he visited. **new opera House:** Chicago was quite the mecca for opera, and the Crosby Opera House, on the north side of Washington Street between State and Dearborn, had opened in April of 1865. It was indeed a grand theater, seating three thousand, and cost six hundred thousand dollars to build. **"Norma":** The Italian Opera Company opened its 1865 Chicago season on June 3 with Charles Gounod's *Faust,* followed by Vincenzo Bellini's *Norma,* Daniel Auber's *Fra Diavolo,* Giuseppe Verdi's *Sicilian Vespers* (thus advertised in English), and *La forza del destino.* Since early-nineteenth-century opera houses were not plunged into the stygian darkness we experience today, W could have easily followed the plot with a libretto purchased at the box office.

Wednesday 7 My report of the court and my "Opera" appeared this morning in the *Tribune*. Called at the office and received rather a cold shoulder. Went away and called at the Times office. Was treated cordially and given great encouragement. Am to call again in the morning. My credentials please, and the Chief says he has seen my locals in the 'Tiser. Felt a little more encouraged, and went to the Fair in the evening with quite a light heart. O! if I can only succeed!

My report: For a list of W's Chicago newspaper articles, see Appendix B. W's discomfort with the weather is apparent from the opening sentence of his opera review: "The atmosphere last evening was sultry, yet it was not exceedingly warm at the Opera." **Times office:** on the south side of Randolph Street, between State and Dearborn streets. **'Tiser:** *The Oswego Commercial Advertiser and Times,* where W had worked as a local reporter from January 18 to May 17, 1865. When he left, he obtained letters of recommendation from the mayor, an alderman, and various other important figures in Oswego. **Fair:** The Soldiers' Fair (officially known as the Second Sanitary Fair), was a fund-raising event

Crosby's Opera House. Most of the ground floor was given over to musical-instrument dealers and the music publishing firm of Root and Cady, but Kinsley's restaurant can be seen to the right of the entrance. From James W. Sheahan's *Chicago Illustrated* (1866).

that had opened June 1 and featured, among other attractions, Lincoln's famous log cabin.

Thursday 8 At the Times office early and was set to work reporting a great and disastrous fire which occurred last night. Made a very lengthy report of it—and it seemed to please well. Wrote several other small items. ¶Everything seems to look bright now. The Times men seem pleased with me, and Surely I am with them. Will do my very best, and pray for success—success on which not only my own happiness depends. Around town in evening.

Friday 9 Wrote up somewhat lengthy article on the late fire and its results, which I have not yet seen printed, and conclude was rejected. Wrote several minor articles, and went around the city some. ¶Called on General Sherman at the Tremont House in the evening and had the honor of shaking hands with the hero of Georgia. ¶Met Pardee of Oswego and Seneca Hill memory, at the Sherman House in evening. He agreed to stay with me to-morrow night.

Sherman: William Tecumseh Sherman (1820–91) was in Chicago to appear at the Soldiers' Fair. **Tremont House:** On the southeast corner of Dearborn and Lake streets, it was rebuilt by Ira Couch in 1851 after several fires had destroyed the earlier hotels there. Couch is still recognized in Chicago for the mausoleum in Lincoln Park north of the Chicago Historical Society that bears his last name. **Sherman House:** The newest incarnation (after several fires) opened in 1861 on northwest corner of Clark and Randolph. In 1865 it was managed by John A. Rice, David Gage, and Charles C. Waite. **Pardee:** a fellow member of W's Upsilon Beta (YB) fraternity.

Saturday 10 Up at five o'clock, took train and went to Laporte, Indiana, there met the train bringing General Grant, Mrs. and staff to Chicago. Rode back in the state car, made the acquaintance of the parties, and drunk the General's wine and smoked his cigars. Only think of it! Jack Wing of Holmesville riding, smoking and drinking with Gen'l Grant, the hero of America. Wrote a report of what I saw and heard, which was very much indeed. All over town on business in eve. ¶Rec'd $9 from the office in an envelope, so I conclude I am to have $18 per week.

Grant: Ulysses S. Grant (1822–85) was also traveling to Chicago to appear at the Soldiers' Fair. W's trip to Indiana to catch Grant's train was typical of his initiative in getting a news story. The meeting with General Sherman the night before was also probably an attempt to get a news story, but no reports by W on either general appeared at this time in the *Times*.

Sunday 11 Remained in my little, hot, 7′ by 9′ room all the fore-noon, and slept fitfully. Never suffered so much by the heat before in my life. It is absolutely killing. ¶After dinner went to the office, and walked around some. Back to the room, armed with a bottle of ink, and wrote eight letters; one home, one to John Barry, asking him to notice my connection with the Times in the Palladium. ¶At the office in the evening, and wrote several items. Went to bed tired out.

dinner: W means a large midday meal, a common usage; the evening meal was referred to as supper. W also refers to supper as "tea." **Palladium:** another Oswego newspaper.

Monday 12 Reported at the office very early in the morning. Was assigned a great task, that of going to Camp Fry and writing an article upon it. Found my way there, and made all the enquiries possible. Returned and wrote an article which would make a whole local page in the 'Tiser. In the afternoon reported the Board of Education, and did much else. Left the office late, and retired very tired indeed with my days work; but rejoicing that at length I am settled.

Camp Fry: Built in 1863 as a camp for Illinois Union recruits, it was converted into a prisoner-of-war camp in 1864. The camp was some three miles from the city center at what is now the intersection of Clark, Diversey, and Broadway. Perhaps W "found" his way there because it was beyond the northern city limit of Fullerton Avenue.

Tuesday 13 Whoever thought that I should be hard at work on the greatest copperhead paper in the whole country. Such is the case nevertheless. i am quite fond of my place, as it offers great cultivation, and pays pretty well. If I can only fill it, that's the point. Obtained another room at the St. Cloud, quite large, three windows, and furnished with a new set of furniture throughout. In point of furniture it is the best room I ever had. Nine dollars a week is the swindle upon it.

copperhead: northern sympathizers of the southern secessionists during the Civil War. In his teens, W was a staunch Republican and had been an ardent supporter of Abraham Lincoln.

Wednesday 14 Went to the police court at 8 o'clock and lingered through its tedious session. Beheld the usual amount of crime and suffering. Cannot help contrast[ing] this and the Oswego court. Old Harman all patience and practice, this judge petulant and ignorant. Wrote a gossipy article upon it & several small items. ¶Visited Camp Fry again and wrote a somewhat lengthy article upon the regiment encamped there. A very busy day, as in fact all the days in this office are. But I prefer it to Oswego any day.

Thursday 15 One week as a Reporter on the Chicago Daily

Times. It has been a momentous week to me. Things that I never dreamed of have passed before my vision, and I am getting to be quite at home in this great metropolis of the west. I have made my mark here by getting business where thousands fail. ¶At the police court in the morning and wrote a gossipy article upon it and several small items. At the great billiard tournament in the evening, copying a speech.

Friday 16 Went up North Clark Street in the morning to look after a fire, and wrote a lengthy article upon it. Looking after the different regiments that are arriving, which is the hardest work in the office. Up to the Turner's Hall very late in the night, and reported the reception to the Hecker regiment. The hottest place I was ever in. Footed it down about midnight, and wrote up a long report. Did not get to bed until about 3 o'clock. This smacks of work upon the old Herald.

Turner's Hall: north of the Chicago River on the west side of Clark Street between Chicago and Chestnut streets. **Hecker regiment:** so named after the German-born Friedrich Karl Franz Hecker (1811–81), colonel in the Union Army and commander of the 82nd Illinois regiment. **Herald:** the *Utica Morning Herald,* where W had worked as a night-shift proofreader and editor from 1/27/6 to 1/16/65.

Saturday 17 At the Fair in the morning, reporting Gen'l. Sherman's movements. Looked after regiments and reported the sale of seats in Crosby Opera House in the afternoon. ¶Rec'd a letter—my first in Chicago—from Divine, in regard to the grand Circle Convention. Brad has had a "blow out" with Thomson and left 'Tiser; so I am not alone in having rows with bosses. ¶Rec'd $18, which I conclude is to be my salary—the largest I ever got. Was measured for a new sack coat which cost $20.

Divine: B. C. Divine, a fellow YB member. **grand Circle Convention:** an Upsilon Beta meeting to be held on November 14th and 15th. **sack coat:** a loose-fitting man's coat, single or double breasted, for informal wear.

Sunday 18 Slept nearly all the forenoon. Then up and enjoyed the first wash since left Oswego; put on a white shirt, and felt much more like myself than when sweltering under my linens. Tried my new boots and they fairly kill me every step I take.

¶Down to office and Soldier's Rest in afternoon. Back and had a good sleep, then wrote letters to Kenyon, Copeland and Dr. Swan. ¶Very dull in the evening. Went to office and then came back and went to bed at an early hour. ¶"So goes the world" with me now!

first wash: must refer to W's first full bath since leaving Oswego. **new boots:** W had perpetual problems with ill-fitting shoes. The topic occurs frequently in his diaries. **Soldier's Rest:** Opened on January 22, 1864, this was a place for sick and wounded soldiers, as well as soldiers in transit to and from the war, where they were given a bed and hot meals. During the first two weeks of June 1865, 7,048 soldiers passed through its facilities and ate 11,063 meals. In the fall of 1865, the Soldier's Rest became the Soldier's Home. The original 1864 building still stands at 739 E. 35th Street, south of the Stephen A. Douglas Monument. **Kenyon, Copeland and Dr. Swan:** friends from upstate New York.

Monday 19 Followed the Hecker regiment around all the morning. About noon an awful explosion occurred in the river, a tug boat. Was sent to write it up, and spent nearly all the afternoon in doing so. Wrote about a column upon it. ¶Wrote up the doings of the regiment in the evening, and also several small items. Went down to the fair after the receipts and stayed there until midnight. Then wrote them out, and got to bed at one o'-clock.

receipts: the income from the Soldiers' Fair. By its end, the fair had grossed $358,070. Some of the net receipts were used to support the Soldier's Rest.

Tuesday 20 My very long and bully account of the tug boat explosion appears this morning, and reads bully. ¶Went around to the tug boat offices, the police station, the fair, etc., and picked up infinitesimal items. Wrote nothing of any great account, of course. ¶After the fair receipts in the evening and to bed very late. ¶Attempted to wear my new boots, but the effort is [in] vain. And so I have made another failure. $13 out, and not a cent in!

Wednesday 21 In morning wrote an article headed "Lager on the decline," and several minor articles. ¶Goodsel[l] told me that I must go to South Bend, Ind., 85 miles distant, to report the commencement exercises of the University of Notre Dame—a large

Catholic Institution. Got a pass, and started at five o'clock. Had my new boots on and they pinched me terribly. After a hard ride arrived at South Bend. Hotels all full. Slept on the floor in a rookery with a stranger. Another western adventure.

"**Lager on the decline":** Part of W's fortune would be made from his publications, *The Western Brewer* (1876–87) and *Wing's Brewers' Handbook of the United States and Canada* (1877–84), trade journals for the beer industry. **Goodsel:** It is hard to say which Goodsell W refers to here, so many of them worked on the paper; John was the general editor, James H. was the city editor, and Charles M. the local (regional) editor of the *Times*. Here, it may be Charles, but W would soon work for James. See 6/26/65 and 7/9/65. During his stay at the *Times*, W's articles appeared in both the city and local news columns. **University of Notre Dame:** The university was founded in 1842 by the Order of the Holy Cross.

Thursday 22 Up before breakfast and drove over to the University. The Brotherhood of the Holy Cross "are a set of cusses.["] Never was treated so bountiful in my life. Cigars, wine, everything one could possibly hope for. Was showed through the most delightful grounds I ever saw in my life. Wrote 51 pages of report. Gen'l Sherman was there and family. Had a splendid time. Got through with a pocket full of havanas and took cars for home. Arrived in Chicago at midnight with my report all written.

Friday 23 If my experience with the Catholics yesterday be anything of a criterion by which to judge of them, I am sure that my opinion of them is much improved. I never before saw such real munificence. Notre Dame is a lovely place—I trust I may visit it again. ¶Wrote out my report in the evening and enlarged upon it. Wrote several items in the afternoon. Went to Col. Wood's in the evening, and the fair.

Col. Wood's: Wood's Theatre and Museum was on the north side of Randolph Street between Clark and Dearborn and had opened in August 1863. It featured natural science exhibits, an art gallery, a panorama of the City of London, and a theater. Originally run by John O'Mellen and others, Col. Wood became its owner in 1864. W may have seen *Leap Year; or, The Ladies' Privilege,* a three-act comedy by the prolific English-born playwright John Buckstone (1802–79); *A Grand Dance* [performed] *by Miss Jenny Hight*; and a two-act comedy, *Breach of Promise; or, Second Thoughts Are Best,* also by Buckstone.

Col. Wood's Theatre and Museum. To the left of the Colonel's is Baker's Wood Engraving Company, where W would have his stock-yard map prepared. Two doors to the right is the Matteson House, whose bar W frequented and where he would stay in the fall of 1866. From James W. Sheahan's *Chicago Illustrated* (1866).

Saturday 24 If ever I get another tight pair of boots may I have corns on every toe. Traded off my boots for a pair of shoes and paid $5.00 to boot—making the shoes cost me $18.00. And when I had bot [bought] the shoes they were also too small—and I had to get them back and ordered another pair. O feet! ¶Recd. a letter from Annie enclosing one from Edson who tenders his resignation as Grand Secretary of the Upsilon Beta Society. What will become of it!?

Annie: Anna Wing, his younger sister, was born in 1848.

Sunday 25 Spent the forenoon in bed. Put on my new suit of clothes which suit me very much. Sold my over coat, gray under coat and pants to a Jew for $18, but was obliged to do it to get the others. ¶Out to Camp Douglas in afternoon and got roster of the 93d Regiment. ¶Wrote letters to all the different YB Chapters informing them of Edson's resignation and calling the convention the 9th of August. Loafing in evening. Wrote up account of 93d. Sent Annie $4.00 by letter.

Camp Douglas: a military camp for Illinois regiments, built in 1861. It was roughly between 31st and 33rd streets and Forest and Cottage Grove Avenue. By the winter of 1861–62, it began serving as a prison for Confederate soldiers. After the war, it was a camp for returning Union soldiers.

Monday 26 At the office early and wrote up article on the incidents of the late storm, also a seduction case and several others. ¶Goodsell told me that they would probably want me to go to work in the news department as they must reduce the local force. Don't know what to make of this! It may mean that I will soon be shipped altogether. Can hardly believe it however. ¶Bronk from Hamilton College asked me to lend him $5. He is awful hard up. Lent him all I had—70 cents.

shipped: got rid of. **Bronk:** a YB member from upstate N.Y.

Tuesday 27 A busy day. The first thing in the morning wrote an article on the Immigration to the West, which was printed under a big head. Also wrote a side head article entitled "On the River." ¶Was detailed to report the commencement of the "University of St. Mary's on the Lake." Made nearly a column report of it. Had some fine "Catawba" with the President and Professors. Have made up my mind since Notre Dame affair that the Catholics are a bully set after all.

"Catawba": wine made from catawba grapes.

Wednesday 28 Spent a terribly hot morning by an excursion to the North Pier after a "crib" item, which of course I got. Wrote a lengthy article on "Early Fruit," which was printed with a big head. Went to the Armory in the afternoon and wrote several articles and items on what I saw there. At Col. Woods' Museum a bit in the evening. ¶John Fitzgerald is in town from Oswego. Invited him to dinner with me, for the report he will carry to Oswego will pay me well for cozening him.

Armory: On the southeast corner of Adams and Market (now Wacker), it contained the Police Justices' courts and a holding jail for those awaiting trial.

Thursday 29 At the Armory in the morning. Made a dollar by keeping a fellow's name out of the paper "which I had no idea of putting in." Lucky. ¶Wrote an article on the "Tricks of Trade" which created quite a sensation. ¶Started for Wau-kegan at 5:20 to Report the Execution of Wm. Bell, the murderer. Arrived there, met Wright of the Republican. A cuss from the Tribune tried to euchre us, but failed signally. Saw the gallows, talked with "the doomed man." Called on Sheriff and his minister. Spent half the night at his cell. Wrote until 3 o'clock.

Tricks: W's article related how clothing merchants attempted to lure returning veterans into their stores with window displays of military badges, portraits of Lincoln, and other patriotic goods. There was a demand for civilian clothes after the war, and competition among tradesmen was fierce. **met Wright:** Charles H. Wright. **euchre:** probably "scoop." See 7/20/65.

Friday 30 O! long to be remembered day. Up and breakfasted. Saw the man who had but a few hours to live. Heard the minister pray with him. It was awful. Wrote until 2 o'clock and then gathered at the gallows with the witnesses of the execution. It was awful. The man talked an hour on the gallows, then his shroud was put on, then the cap. He protested his innocence to the last breath. O! it was an awful sight—may I never see another. In an instant he was launched into eternity. What if he were innocent, as I believe he was. ¶Returned and wrote up a 4 column report.

JULY

Saturday 1 My report of the execution is nearly four columns long and the best report that was made. Tribune's is heavy and devoid of incident. ¶Did not do much in the forenoon. Went out to Camp Douglas in the afternoon and reported the arrival of the 92 Rgt [Regiment]. ¶When I got my pay I recd. $20 instead of $18, so I conclude that my salary has been raised. Am confident that I suit well. O! how lucky for me. Was paid $4.00 for my expenses, double what they were.

The Armory. On the southeast corner of Adams and Market (now Wacker), it contained the Police Justices' courts and a holding jail for those awaiting trial. From James W. Sheahan's *Chicago Illustrated* (1866).

Sunday 2 Did not wake until noon and was late at dinner. Enjoyed a good smoke and then went to go to the office. Met Philip and he enticed me out to Wright's Garden where the afternoon was spent. Had a very lousy time indeed. Did not write anything as I have done Sunday work ever since I have been here. ¶How marvelously I am getting along. O! to think of those awful hours and days I spent after the Brigham affair! Now I have such a splendid place. Surely time and effort work wonders for me.

Philip: W never gives the last name of this assistant city editor of the *Times*, nor have I been able to trace him. See 7/10/65. **Wright's Garden:** perhaps a beer garden connected with Wright's Hotel at 22–24 North Wells Street or Wright & Leonard's Dining Hall at 83 South Clark Street. It is also possible that W has miswritten Garden for Grove, which would place it near Camp Fry in an area known as Wright's Grove. **Brigham:** T. S. Brigham, the publisher and editor of the *Oswego Commer-*

cial Advertiser. He had fired W from his position as local reporter in May of 1865.

Monday 3 Went to Armory in the morning and wrote nearly half a column upon police officer. Reported the return of Battery A. ¶Goodsell out of town and [I] did not work very hard. The evening, however, was rather an exciting time. Went to a banquet at the Revere House. While there a fire broke out adjoining, which destroyed a whole block of buildings. Fell in with a bully little boy whom I cozzened some in hope I may meet again ere long. Went to bed late.

Revere House: a hotel on the northeast corner of Clark and Kinzie streets. **cozzened:** not in the usual sense of "to cheat or defraud" but "to chat or talk with," probably with an eye toward some eventual real or imagined gain. Cf. W's use of "cozening" on 6/28/65.

Tuesday 4 The Fourth! ¶Spent the morning in looking at the procession and the afternoon in hearing Henry Winter Davis speak. ¶Went to the fireworks on Michigan Avenue in the evening. Was very tired and fatigued. Dropped into Kinsly's and run against Frank Marvin and Bob Tyrrel who had been looking for me nearly all the afternoon. It was a glad moment for me. Frank went and stayed with me. He is a bully boy and I love him much. His acquaintance will prove valuable.

Henry Winter Davis: (1817–65) A Maryland Republican representative to the U.S. Congress (1863–65), opposed to Lincoln's plan for Reconstruction. **Kinsly's:** Kinsley's Restaurant, operated by Herbert M. Kinsley at 65 Washington Street on the ground floor of Crosby's Opera House. **Marvin:** a friend W made in Detroit on June 2, 1865. **Tyrrel:** a YB from Utica, N.Y., whom W had also run into in Detroit just before his arrival in Chicago.

Wednesday 5 Left the boys by themselves during the day and worked as usual. Wrote a lengthy article on the Spiritualists at Waukegan, and the soul of Bell, the murderer. Also several small articles. Reported the Board of Education in the evening, which lasted until midnight. Met Frank and Bob at Kinsly's and after a dish of [ice] cream they went to the St. Cloud with me and stayed over night, Frank and I again sleeping together. Frank is a stylish cub and my love for him increaseth.

July 1865

Thursday 6 Left the boys to breakfast at Thomas's and went to office. Wrote a long article upon a public park which was published entire. Also visited the jail and wrote an article entitled "Behind the Bars," "The demireps in prison," etc. Besides this wrote "Much Ado About Nothing." ¶Went to the Lake Tunnel in the afternoon with Frank and Bob. We entered the "great bore." Went out to Camp Douglas and reported the 57th Rgt. The boys went to stay with me again, but Bob flunked and went elswhere.

demireps: A euphemism for prostitutes. **Lake Tunnel:** City water had become nearly undrinkable by 1863, and a project was proposed by the city engineer, Ellis S. Chesbrough, to dig a tunnel out into Lake Michigan to obtain clean water. After taking bids the Harrisburg, Pa., firm of Dull and Gowan was chosen to do the job and construction began on St. Patrick's Day, 1864. The digging of the two-mile tunnel under the lake from the shore to an offshore crib was completed in December of 1866 and put into service on March 25, 1867. During its construction, the tunnel proved to be a great tourist attraction as well as an engineering marvel, and tours through it were given to visiting dignitaries such as General U. S. Grant (see 8/16/65). W would publish a pamphlet on the Lake Tunnel in 1866, a revised edition in 1867, and reprints in 1868 and 1874. See 11/28/66 et seq. for this project. **reported the 57th Rgt.:** W is behind in his diary. The 57th Illinois Regiment did not arrive in Chicago until the 8th. **flunked:** backed out.

Friday 7 Goodsell sent me to get up a market [report] in the forenoon, which I found to be anything but a desirable job. Old Story wanted to see me and desired that I should take a position on the news department. Promised him I would and feel rather elated. ¶While reporting police commissioners in the afternoon, Bob and Frank came to bid me adieu, which I did then with much feeling, this being the only familiar faces I have met in Chicago. To Col. Woods in eve.

Old Story: Wilbur Fisk Storey (1819–84), editor and publisher of the *Chicago Times*. **Woods:** Playing at Col. Wood's were *Breach of Promise; or, Second Thoughts Are Best* (see 6/23/65) and *The Serious Family*, an English adaptation by Morris Barnett (1800–56) of the French comedy *Un Mari en Champaigne* (also known as *Le Mari à la Campagne*) by Bayard and Voirly.

Saturday 8 A day which proved very eventful to me. ¶Wrote a long article upon a Soldier's Monument and one upon a garrulous parrott, in the morning. ¶In the afternoon went out to camp of gypsys and wrote over a column on them, which was the best article I have yet written, and which led to results hereafter to be seen. Also reported a regiment; making in all over two columns and a half of matter—twice what any other man on the paper wrote. Set up for almost until 3 o'c.

a Soldier's Monument: W's article was a proposal to raise money for the erection of a monument to the Union soldiers. **hereafter to be seen:** This phrase suggests that W had fallen behind in his diary entries, although he sometimes uses it in anticipation of some future event.

Sunday 9 Up at an early hour for Sun. breakfasted and went to the office to see my article on the gypsys. Found Goodsell there, and was complimented for it. He then wanted me to refuse the position in the news department, and take the position of assistant city editor, which I decided to do. He expressed himself greatly pleased with me. O! success, success!!!—!!! ¶Wrote a joyful letter home, telling of my great fortune. At the office in the evening, and wrote several items. Feeling bully!

Monday 10 Philip, the sweet scented, started for Detroit, and I made preparations to assume his posishin. Employed the forenoon in writing upon different topics, as they suggested themselves. ¶Commenced work in the evening as assistant city editor of THE CHICAGO TIMES, a position to which I never even aspired. It was rather a rough initiation as there was a lengthy report of the Common council in a very muchly boluxed condition. Wrote an enormous sensation article very late, on "A Child dying in its Mothers arms" etc, with an enormous head.

Tuesday 11 If anything goes amiss here, I am not treated in the manner which old El Roberts treated me of yore, when I was laboring and wearing out my very life for him without recompense. There were a few slight mistakes in my work last evening, but they will be righted next time. ¶A horrible stabbing affray occurred, which Chas—"my brother" took in hand, knowing that he could manage it as it deserved. Wrote several sensation items in the morning. ¶Purchased some rare old french books at an old bookstore, for 10¢ apiece—worth more for stock.

El Roberts: Ellis H. Roberts, publisher and editor of the *Utica Morning Herald,* where W had worked in 1864. **Chas:** Charles Aug was a fellow reporter and rival on the *Times*. W's quotes around "my brother" are probably sarcastic. **french books:** This is W's first purchase of books purely as artifacts, since he knew only a few common words and phrases in French. He may have bought them at Edward Buehler's Clark Street bookstore, which specialized in German and French books.

Wednesday 12 Wrote a long article upon the thieves room at the Central Station, which will make quite a sensation. Also one on home gossip. In the evening wrote several articles, and got along with the work splendidly—better than I could even hope to. ¶Received a letter from Lon Kenyon and one from Frank Marvin. Bob Tyrrel lost his situation by stopping so long in Chicago—his stay was certainly not my fault. ¶Met Andrew Clark, an old Boonville friend. "History ever repeats itself."

Lon Kenyon: a longtime friend of W's from Oswego, N.Y.

Thursday 13 Called to see Miss Fransted, the fancy woman so badly stabbed by the jealous wife. Investigated the case, and wrote a lengthy article upon it, introducing some little gossip. ¶The day passed without any very great exertion on my part. Had Phillip's old case cleaned out, and proceeded to make myself comfortable in his old position. ¶Am succeeding more than well here. O! if I could have known, when the horrible Oswego *denoument* occured, how I should come out, how it would have changed my feelings then!

Oswego *denoument*: a reference to W's dismissal from the *Oswego Commercial Advertiser,* the immediate cause of his western migration.

Friday 14 Wrote an addition to the "thieves of Chicago," and several minor articles. Nothing transpired of any moment, out of the usual routine of every day work. Shave after dinner, and then wrote up items from the *Journal,* also an article on the public schools. ¶Considerable to do in the evening, and did not get away until twelve o'clock. Went to Col. Woods a few moments. ¶It seems natural to resume night work again; but how different is it from those terrible nights of suffering on the *Herald*!

night work: See 6/16/65.

Saturday 15 Very dark and rainy day. On way to the office got an item from the coroner. ¶Goodsell is very communicative, and seems to desire to make a sort of *confidante* of me, which I have no objection of him doing, if it will accrue to my advantage. ¶At that rare old bookstore again and purchased several valuable old English works, which the seller cannot possibly know the value of, else he would tripple the price. ¶Things as usual in the evening. Read some.

Sunday 16 Up to breakfast, made toillete and down to the office. My article on "The Thieves of Chicago" appears, making nearly a column, and reading very well. Also my article on "Summer Recreation." ¶Slept in afternoon, and then wrote three letters—to Frank Marvin, to Lon Kenyon, and one to old Brigham, setting forth my new position, and politely informing him, "that as I owed it to his difficulty, I thanked God that he was the meanest man living." Something may come of it—hope there will.

Brigham: T. S. Brigham. See 7/2/65.

Monday 17 Stayed at the office very late last night. Wrote an article on the "Ships of Chicago" plagarizing a little from Leigh Hunt. At work at an early hour this morning. Wrote a sensation on a somnambulist and several other things. ¶Goodsell says that when I am permanently settled in my present position that I shall get $25 per week salary. Therefore I am anxious to get settle. ¶If that lucky day ever comes, then bully for me. But I think it is at hand.

Leigh Hunt: (1784–1859). British writer and editor (1806–21) of the *Examiner.*

Tuesday 18 Did very little in the forenoon excepting an article on "The transgressions of War Widows," Which was a crim. con. of the first water. ¶In the afternoon Goodsell went home sick, and I had the whole charge of things. Sent up my article on the streets, and one entitled "an Indigo Bath." In the evening several other things came up. So that I shall get out a big paper in the morning. ¶Dropped into Col. Wood's theatre in the evening, and was much pleased with the play.

crim. con.: criminal conviction. **play:** *Camilla's Husband,* a drama by Watts Phillips (1825–74); on the bottom half of the bill was *The Widow's Victim,* a one-act farce by Charles Selby (1802?–63). W must have really liked *Camilla's Husband,* as he saw it again on 7/22/65 and perhaps on 7/28/65.

Wednesday 19 Wrote an article upon the "Sanitary Reform," which Goodsell complimented me for. Also one upon the Gift enterprises. ¶The evening, or rather night, was a busy one. Dropped into Bryant & Stratton's Festival in the evening, and got some ice cream. ¶An Alarm of fire at midnight, soon followed by another and still another. Sent Chisholm & Hanson to them. Jim [Chisholm] returned very late, & he sent up a rousing report; and did not get to bed until four o'clock.

Gift enterprises: This was a court case in which the owners of "gift enterprise stores" were convicted and fined for running an illegal lottery. **Bryant & Stratton's:** a national chain of business colleges in fifty cities. The Chicago college was on the northeast corner of Washington and Clark streets, opposite the City Court House. **Chisholm & Hanson:** James C. Chisholm and —? Hanson, *Times* reporters. See also 8/1/65. The Scottish-born Chisholm (b. 1838) had migrated to Chicago in 1864.

Thursday 20 Did not get up to breakfast; but took a plate of soup at Franks. Found that we had euchered the other papers. Goodsell was greatly pleased, or so expressed himself. ¶Went out into the lake with Col. Gowan's lake tunnel party in the afternoon, to make observations. Had quite a little excursion. ¶In the evening Old Story came down in a towering rage, about a large ~~age~~ copy, about which I knew nothing. ¶Went home and to bed about 10 'clock, very tired.

euchered: Here it clearly means "scooped." **Col. Gowan:** James Gowan, supervising engineer of the Chicago lake tunnel project. See 7/6/65. **large copy:** a long article.

Friday 21 An eventful day. News came to the office in the morning that a terrible riot was taking place on the north side. I hastened to the spot, found a soldier shot, and a building demolished. Returned to the office and wrote 44 paragraphs [upon] it. It was a very big thing. (See report in Scrap book.) ¶Sent up a large amount of copy in the evening; but got through and went to bed about 12 o'clock. ¶Recd box containing my tile [hat] from home.

a terrible riot: This occurred near the corner of Wells and Kinzie streets and involved an Iowa regiment returning from the war.

Saturday 22 In the morning wrote a lengthy article upon Mrs Livermore and Mrs Hoge, which is calculated to make quite a sensation. Also one entitled "Flies, Flies, Flies![''] which suits me bully. ¶Goodspeed out of town, and left me in charge. Every thing goes off well. Dropped into Col. Wood's in the evening, to see Camille, a new play. ¶Recd a letter from Kenyon. Cud Swan was to arrive there to-day. Wish I could see the boy. What a history is his!!

Mrs Livermore and Mrs Hoge: Mrs. Mary A. Livermore and Mrs. A. H. Hoge were prominent in various city charitable organizations. This article was about a dispute in the executive committee of the Soldier's Rest. **Goodspeed:** miswriting for Goodsell. **Camille:** See 7/18/65. **Cud Swan:** Charles Swan, a friend from Rome, N.Y.

Sunday 23 Having forgotten to inform Chisholm last evening that he was to go to a meeting at Bridgeport to-day, I hastened up to breakfast in the morning and then to the office. My article on the Sanitary Committe reads bully. It's a big thing. Could not find Jim and sent Hanson to the meeting. ¶Got wind of a big raid by the police—capture of 200 gamblers. Went to the armory, found it true, wrote over a column, had a row with the printers about their names give etc, etc, as they were in the party pulled. A big thing.

armory: The penultimate sentence is nearly illegible and unintelligible, but since the news article printed all the names of those arrested in the raid, W must have had an argument with the printers about including these names.

Monday 24 Up very early; went to the office and sent the reporters out; and took the launch of the great tunnel crib myself.

¶It was a fine sight. Went out on a tug with Gov. Oglesby's party. Returned to dinner. Got to the office at three o'clock, and wrote over three columns on the launch, which was printed with cuts of the tunnel. ¶Supervised all the copy in the evening, and wrote a sensation article. The biggest and hardest day's work I have done in my life. Very fatigued.

Oglesby: Richard James Oglesby (1824–99), Republican governor of Illinois (1864–68). **cuts:** wood-engraved illustrations. W's piece on the tunnel was printed on the front page with pictures, a rare instance of an illustrated article in the *Times.*

Tuesday 25 After my hard day's work of yesterday, did not hurry about getting to the office. Neither did I write very much when there. ¶Made a small paragraph on "Don Juan de Casta" and several minor items. ¶Purchased an exceedingly quaint old book at bookstall for $1, which I can ill afford; but my antiquarian propensities ran away with me. Wish that I could afford to buy a few more that I have my eye on. ¶Went to the theatre a few moments in the evening.

Wednesday 26 Wrote an article on "Negro Immigration" in which I said many things against my belief, now that I am selling my brains to a copperhead paper. Also an article on "The Rush to Chicago." ¶Purchased several books, among them "The Thieves Jargon," an invaluable little thing for which I paid $1. ¶Recd a letter from Devine, saying that the Utica boys had sold out the old lodge, and would not have the convention there. Wrote him a pretty rough letter in reply. Also wrote to Charley Gurley at Quincy. A hard night's work.

against my belief: W favored abolition. **"The Thieves Jargon":** perhaps a pamphlet from an article by this title on British underworld slang that had appeared in *Harper's New Monthly Magazine,* April 1865 (pp. 601–6). **Devine:** W's variant spelling of Divine. See 6/17/65. **Charley Gurley:** W's best boyhood friend in Pulaski, N.Y., where they both attended the Pulaski Academy. Gurley had migrated to Quincy, Ill., in 1864 to work in a bank.

Thursday 27 It is highly probable that the press of business upon my time will cause this veracious diary to get so far behind in its records that the sight [of it will] cause me to abandon it.

However that may be, if this should turn out [to be] the last page, let not posterity blame me, but business. ¶There has [been] nothing very unusual [that has] transpired to-day. Chicago is awfull[y] full of excitement but it seldom gets on a tear, like smaller cities. To-day it has maintained the even tenor of its ways, and so live I.

Friday 28 More rush for matter to-day than for time. Nothing to write upon, and the necessity for writing something binding. ¶Wrote several items from subject suggested by the meeting of the common council last evening, among them "Who Pays the Drinks" etc. ¶It is not nown [?], at the writing of this neglected diary, which is two weeks behind, it being the 12th of August as I write, what Jack Wing did in the evening of this day. But judging from his habits it is fair to infer that he went to the theatre.

nown: The word is rather illegible, but "known" makes sense in this context. **theatre:** W's choices would have been *Camilla's Husband* and *The Widow's Victim*, still playing at Wood's, or Budworth's Minstrels at the Academy of Music. Crosby's was dark this Friday.

Saturday 29 A very dull evening and strong indications of a dull day and a poor local to-morrow. Went On 'Change in the forenoon, and observed the motions of the speculatres. Wrote a lengthy article on it. ¶Wrote a lengthy article on the opera in Chicago comparing it with New York (a place which of course I am perfectly familiar with, and have been for five years, ever since I learned to lie.). ¶My usual evening work supervising copy etc.; and to bed late.

'Change: Chicago Stock Exchange. **five years:** W is referring to his work on newspapers, where he began as a printer's devil in April of 1860.

Sunday 30 The usual Sabbath day exercises and loneliness. Went to the office and got a paper; returned to the St Cloud and lay around until noon. Wrote letters in afternoon, slept, and it was night before I knew it. ¶Philip—the sweet scented vase that smells though broken—has returned. I feel that the crown of asst. City Ed. sits heavily and uneasily upon my head. I imagine it already gone. He assumes it [is] his as a matter of course. To-morrow will tell whether Goodsell means to keep his word or not.

Monday 31 How many, many times have I been obliged to write at the head of these pages, "An Eventful Day?" This was a more painful one to me than I have yet experienced. ¶In the afternoon I found sweet scented Philip writing at my case. I soon receive a letter from Goodsell saying that he "could not justly displace him" and that I could make my contemplated trip to Quincy if I desired. Strange to say I did not *desire*! Philip ordered me to a picnic—told him I should not go. Took home all my effects, and with an aching heart. Goodsell, of course, had obliged his cowardly spirit and gone home to avoid the blast.

AUGUST

Tuesday 1 At the office very early, desiring to confront Goodsell, and at once learned my fate. He palavers with all the low drivel of a dog, and desires me to stay; saying that I shall have $25 per week, etc. I could do no other. So taking a table, from which poor Hanson was discharged on Sat. I went to work. And here ends my first broil in THE TIMES office. ¶Wrote a lengthy burlesque on the Nigger picnic taking place to-day. One would think to read it that I had turned Copperhead, and was the bitterest of the bitter.

Nigger picnic: more likely an expression of sarcasm than personal prejudice, as the following sentence indicates. The picnic was not held by former U.S. slaves but rather was a celebration of the seventeenth anniversary of West Indian emancipation.

Wednesday 2 In the paper this morning appears "A Dusky Occasion" and "Professional Thieves," of mine, both lengthy articles. ¶Wrote a long article headed "Lake View Avenue Drive." ¶In the afternoon made an excursion to the tunnel crib, with the Mayor and several Aldermen, and wrote an article upon it. ¶A great raid was made upon the ~~pack~~ thieves of Wells Street by the police. Went to the armory and got an article upon the subject.

the Mayor: John B. Rice (1809–74), Republican mayor of Chicago from

1865 to 1867. This Maryland-born former actor also built the city's first theater in 1847.

Thursday 3 Wrote a comical article upon "A Great Raid upon Cattle," and also wrote up the arrival of some regiments. ¶Went to a german Concert at Melm's garden in the evening, and wrote a long report. ¶Showed my meerschaum [pipe] to ~~to~~ a broker, and made a trade with him for a beautiful gold neck chain, weighting 34 pennyweights. Paid him $25, to boot, every cent I had in God's world. Then I get $25 for the pipe, the chain being worth $50. All I now want to complete a delightful rig, is a gold watch, which I will soon have.

Melm's garden: A German summer theater located at Chestnut and Clark streets. **broker:** pawnbroker. W would have sporadic recourse to pawnbrokers during his Chicago stay. He even wrote an article on them for the *Times* a week later. **34 pennyweights:** about 1.7 ounces.

Friday 4 Collected data and facts for an article on the "Squatter Settlements of Chicago," at Goodsell's direction. Spent all day in writing it. ¶This article, as the following pages will show, was destined to make more commotion and disturbance in Chicago than any ever printed. It was destined to cause the TIMES more trouble and more loss than any article it ever printed. it was also destined to make Jack Wing tremble in his boots, and carry a six shooter in his pocket night and day.

Saturday 5 As a consequence of my spending all day yesterday on "Squatter Settlements," I did not have a line of matter in the paper this morning. But Goodsell has sent up that article, and the result is confined to the "*Irish.*" But woe be to the Times, as the sequel will show. ¶Wrote several small items, and one of considerable length on the Waukegan murderer, Reuben White. Reported the United Service Club in the evening. ¶Bought several books at my favorite Bookstall. ¶Recd $25 for my salary, the largest I ever received before.

Sunday 6 THE TIMES appears this bright Sabbath morning, and its leading Local article is a column and a half in length on "Squatter Settlements," and all about the squalling and turbulent Irish; who are the only friends, in reality the Times has got, or ought to have. Of course Jack W could not write an article upon the subject without venting a little of his hatred of the bloody, red eyed Irish, so long the supporters of the Dems and the Rebs. And he has at length, unintentionally got a great rap at them, through their own organ, The Chicago Times.

The Times appears: Although there was no official Sunday edition of the *Times* this entry shows that the paper dated Monday, the 7th, came out on Sunday. In reprinting W's article the next day, the *Tribune* confirmed that it had appeared Sunday morning. **"Squatter Settlements":** see Appendix C for this article. According to B. L. Pierce's *History of Chicago*, this article had political repercussions, as it "led to some slight defection from Democratic columns, . . . [which] led to a split in the Irish vote in the election of 1866, and by 1868 a Republican club endeavored to deliver Irish votes in the national election." (Vol. II, p. 15.) **their own organ:** when the *Tribune* ran W's article, it commented that the *Times* was "the organ and special champion of the Emerald element in Chicago, and its principal circulation is obtained among that class. Strike out the patronage derived from the Irish, and the *Chicago Times* would die as speedily as a rat in an air exhausted receiver."

Monday 7 Chandler comes in and says that about 1,000 persons, of the Emerald Isle persuasion have stopped their paper because of my squatter article. Irishmen rush into the office, and threaten to kill the individual who wrote it, if they can only lay hands upon him. The excitement is intense. The Tribune reprints the whole article *verbatim ad litteratium* in this mornings issue, with half a column of editorial. The *Journal* tonight contains an Irish call for an indignation meeting. Things in a nice fix, and Jack Wing patiently awaiting his discharge, and the wrath of Storey.

[Across the page] Afraid of My Little Life.

Chandler: Henry B. Chandler, partner and business manager of the *Times*. **stopped their paper:** The *Chicago Times* nearly went under because of these cancellations and did not fully recover its Irish subscribers for another four months. Six days after W's article appeared, the paper began a series of features meant to gain back the Irish readers. ***Journal*:** *Chicago Evening Journal*.

Tuesday 8 Last night was the first one that I ever carried a revolver, loaded with six saucy looking cartridges. Borrowed one of a friend and stuck as close to it as a brother. Threats of killing me are freely made, and my name has got out. The *Tribune* and *Republican* of this morning contain column editorials on the article and its writer; and a resolution of the Fenians denouncing its writer in the most awful manner. THE TIMES itself contains a weak apology for the article. Tremblingly I await my fate; but laughing in my sleeve.

Fenians: The Fenian Brotherhood, an Irish separatist organization, had its own hall on the northwest corner of Wells and Randolph streets. The American branch was founded in New York in 1856. In 1871 the Irish branch would attempt to assassinate Queen Victoria. **apology:** According to Storey's biographer this was "the only time in the forty-five year career of Wilbur F. Storey his newspaper published an apology" (Walsh, p. 217). Given Storey's predilection for yellow journalism, this is a remarkable statement!

Wednesday 9 Jack Wing never had an idea that his feeble quill could stir up such a quaking, all over a great city. His friends at home would not believe it much. The other papers contain more lengthy editorials, and the Fenians have passed more resolutions. Goodsell thinks that he cannot stand the pressure and "goes East," telling me to go to the Fenian picnic to-morrow, and get my head broke, which I agreed in all sincerity to do. ¶The excitement seems now to have reached its height: but I am not kilt as yet, nor discharged.

Thursday 10 "Misfortunes never come singly." Going to the general delivery to see if there was not a stray letter for me, I recd one from D. Bennet, Justice of the Peace at Utica, N.Y., whom I remember in connection with the Owens-shoes affair. It states that I owe A. Lach jewellers $5 for a *solid* gold ring, which I will remit him at once if I "have the spirits of a man." If I do not do so, it is his intention to "write to my employers, and all editors," informing them of my character, and "if necessary advertise me." Laid the delicate epistle aside, and decided to be published.

Owens-shoes affair: a lawsuit brought against W in January of 1865 in Oswego for his failure to pay for a pair of shoes.

Friday 11 Luckily for me, the Fenian pic~~k~~nic has been postponed, so I can retain my head a few days longer, but not in place by any means. The Squatter excitement continues unabated, and its author is getting very famous. ¶Wrote a lengthy article on the gossip connected with pawn broker's shops, and also one on the terrible tornado, which occurred at South Bend, Ind. on Wednesday. ¶I begin to think I shall live through the squatter affair, as I did through the Battes [?] and several similar ones on the 'Tiser.

Battes: W probably wrote an equally provocative article for the *Oswego Commercial Advertiser.*

Saturday 12 Obtained an advanced proof sheet of Halpin's new directory. Went to work and got up a big article, of about two columns and a half on it. ¶Exchanged my silver watch for a beautiful little gold one. Paid only $15 difference. Think I have struck oil. It's a beauty, and *so* much cheaper than I had expected to get one. Have now got a bully watch and chain. ¶Bought a volume of Scots works, Motherwell's posthumous Poems, Twice Told Tales, Tuckermans Poems, "The Thief," and several other volumes at bookstall for $5.50.

Halpin's new directory: This was the eighth annual edition (1865–66) of the Chicago city and business directory. **Scots . . . Poems:** Walter Scott (1771–1832). It is unclear whether W bought a volume of the collected works of Scott or a collection of works by Scott, and without knowing whether this volume contained prose or poetry, it is impossible to specify the edition. *Posthumous Poems* (1846 or 1848 edition) by William Motherwell (1797–1835). *Twice Told Tales (*1837, 1842, or 1851 edition) by Nathaniel Hawthorne (1804–64). 1860 edition of *Poems* by Frederick Tuckerman (1821–73). **"The Thief":** given W's fondness for English poetry this was probably *The Thief Slain: or the Linen Vail Restored. An heroic-comic poem, in two canto's* by Giles Jacob (1686–1744), London, [1750?].

Sunday 13 The Times contains a page report of the Feinan picnic, an unparalleled specimen of toadyism. Threats are yet openly made by the d—d Irish to slay the author of the Squatter article! but they will be obliged to catch him first. ¶A warm and very disagreeable day. Stopped in my room nearly all day, and wrote several letters. Thoughts of home come ever and anon, to make the day disagreeble. O! for a quiet sabbath once more at home.

Feinan picnic: The *Times* published a *four*-column report of the picnic on 8/14/65. W does not exaggerate that it was "an unparalleled specimen of toadyism." This was the first of many articles featuring the Chicago Irish meant to win them back to the paper.

Monday 14 Did not accomplish overmuch in the forenoon, but worked pretty hard in the afternoon. Monday is a sort of dull day with me always—not because of my having any to do with the females—because the good lord knows that I do nothing of a kind. ¶After I had retired to my v couch, at midnight, Philip came rushing up and said that I must go to Detroit in the morning to meet General Grant's special train. Made all preparations to arise with the lark.

v couch: virtuous couch. W often uses "v" as an abbreviation for virtuous in his diaries.

Tuesday 15 Up at five o'clock and went to the depot and embarked for Detroit, in company with Charley Wright. The day was exceedingly warm and the cars very close. We telegraphed to the superintendent of the road, and soon received permission to board the train. Met it at Ypsilanti and embarked with the great general and his family. The train was a magnificent one—the finest I ever saw. Wrote dispatches on board and telegraphed from every station. Retired at midnight in the same sleeping car that bore the General and his family.

Wright: Charles H. Wright, a reporter for the *Republican* when W met him at the Bell execution on 6/29/65, was now working for the *Times*.

Wednesday 16 Awoke this morning to find the train at Calumet. The General was already up, and the reporters arose and made their toilletes. The magnificent train moved on, and arrived at Chicago half past six o'clock. ¶Purchasing morning papers I found that every one of my dispatches was all sound—and that they read well. ¶In the afternoon wrote up and then went down in the Lake tunnel with Grant's party, and rode out under the lake in a train of cars drawn by a mule.

Thursday 17 This morning my article on the "Ride through the Lake tunnel" appeared, and reads bully; also my article resuming the excursion from Detroit. The former was destined to be

August 1865

largely copied everywhere. ¶Being somewhat weary I desired to rest to-day, but there was no such thing. Left on the 6 o'clock train for Michigan City. Being overtaken by General Grant's engine, I rode to the town with the engineer. The history of the day is recorded in "The Chicago Times." Visited the Penitentiary—saw two men killed—reported the convention, and returned at midnight.

Friday 18 A great day. Joined General Grant's special train for Galena, in company with Sam Medill of the *Tribune*. It was the most magnificent pagent I ever witnessed. Wrote dispatches on the train, and sent one from Freeport. The whole journey was one immense ovation. Arrived at Galena in the afternoon. Wrote and telegraphed a full report of the celebration, & got it through before any of the other fellows. It is recorded in my scrap book. ¶Sam Medill and I occupied a bunk in the five sleeping cars coming back.

Galena: The Ohio-born Grant had moved to Galena with his wife and children to work in a leather store run by his brothers just before the outbreak of the Civil War. **Sam Medill:** Samuel J. Medill (1843–83), brother of the owner of the *Chicago Tribune,* Joseph Medill (1823–99). Sam would become the city editor of the *Tribune* in 1867. The present-day *Tribune*'s interest in baseball might be traced back to Sam Medill, who was one of the founders of the Chicago Baseball Club in 1869.

Saturday 19 Awoke to find the train standing in the Chicago depot. Tremblingly Sam and I made for the offices to see if our dispatches were all right. Rejoiced to find mine so to the letter, but the *Tribune* had failed to receive Sam's, and in consequence had stolen the one I had sent from Freeport. ¶Went to bed very much worn down by my week of travel and excitement. It certainly has been a hard one, but I would like to have it repeated. ¶Felt so much worn out that did not do much work all day.

Sunday 20 Made a somewhat successful effort to recuperate my exhausted energies, by sleeping nearly all day. ¶Wrote letters east in the afternoon, descriptive of my journey with General Grant. And here it may be proper to remark, that the rock bound city of Galena is a proper home for the great man who has just returned there. Nestled among rocky hills, like a stage in the theatre, it is a delightfully picturesque locality. I trust that at some future time I may visit it again, and write it up.

Monday 21 Subject matter for articles, especially in the censation line, being extremely scarce this morning, I amused myself by inventing a horrible tale, from the woman I saw put off of the train on the breakwater the other morning, while going to Michigan City. It made a sta[illegible] sensation, and constituted nearly my entire days work. [Line space] ¶The weeks and days are passing along. Occassionally I hear from home, less frequently from the dear old boys at Utica.

Tuesday 22 Did absolutely nothing in the forenoon. Goodsell is away, and Philip stands in awe of me. ¶Wrote a sensation on a boy run over and a lengthy article upon a Marine disaster. ¶Paid a little attention to Col. Wood's stage in the evening. [Line space] ¶My library increases slowly but surely. I have now about 60 volumes, collected since I came to Chicago, which, put with those at home, would make a good show. I hope some happy day to get them all together.

stage: *The Three Guardsmen,* a stage adaptation of Alexandre Dumas's *Three Musketeers* by Charles Rice (1819–80) was playing.

Wednesday 23 Went out to Des Plaines in the morning to a Camp Meeting. Dined with the happy brethren, and then returned and wrote them a lengthy puff. ¶Chisholm is reporting a big abortion case on the north side. Went over and relieved him. Returning to the office I run against a boy dressed in military clothes, whose countenance was so familiar that I stepped up to him, and succeeded in making his acquaintance by telling him that I must have met him in the south. Invited him to call at the office in the evening, which he did.

Camp Meeting: an outdoor religious gathering. **south:** a ploy, since W had never visited the "south."

Thursday 24 When my newly found soldier boy came to the office last evening, I was charmed by his noble bearing, and the intelligence and refinement which he displayed. Took him to the theatre, and soon became charmed with his society. He went and stayed with me, and my love increased. One thing however, he persisted in doing, which I shall never forget. But I suppose it must have come of army life. His name is Tommy Phelan. ¶Left him a short time in the morning, but he soon returned, and was mine again for the night.

theatre: There was no Wednesday evening performance at Wood's, but the matinee was *Belle's Stratagem,* a three-act comedy by Hannah Cowley (1743–1809), condensed and adapted by Augustin Daly. The McVicker's Theater was playing *Our American Cousin* by Tom Taylor (1817–80), and Budworth's Minstrels were at the Academy of Music. **he persisted in doing:** W is frustratingly uninformative as to what this activity was. **Tommy Phelan:** The only information W gives about this Union veteran was that he claimed to have been a prisoner in Andersonville (see 8/26/65). The only Phelan listed as a prisoner there was Charles *T.* Phelan of the New York 24th Independent Battery Light Artillery. That Phelan first enlisted in Albany, N.Y., into the 24th on September 26, 1861, at the age of eighteen. He was mustered out three months later but reenlisted on January 1, 1864. His entire company was captured at the siege of Plymouth, N.C., on April 20, 1864, and interned at Andersonville, Ga. Paroled in December 1864 from a Charleston, S.C., prison where he had been transferred, Phelan was discharged as a corporal on June 9, 1865, at Annapolis, Md.

Friday 25 Parted with Phalan and went to work, somewhat played out by excess. ¶Wrote gossip about street musicians, and several other items. ¶Took Tommy over to Joe's gallery and had him photographed, for my own gratification. He became enamoured of a servant girl at the St. Cloud, and made an arrangement to take her out in the evening. Left me to go there, and promised to come back, but not being as successful with the female as he hoped, he did not return, and I went to bed alone.

Phalan: Phelan, another example of W's phonetic spelling of names. **Joe's gallery:** Joseph Battersby's photography gallery was on the west side of Clark Street, between Randolph and Lake streets.

Saturday 26 Went to work on a lengthy article on the Chicago river, which I found a very difficult thing to write. Worked very hard all day, and got through about eighty pages, which will make about ~~thre~~ two columns in the local. ¶Tommy came around in the evening, and went to stay with me again, and we had another large time. He starts for Washington to-morrow, being a witness in the Wirtz case, having been a prisoner at Andersonville. ¶What followeth is interesting.

being a witness: According to a contemporary account of the trial of Henry Wirz by Ambrose Spencer, Phelan's military company "was nearly annihilated [in Andersonville] through starvation and disease." Seventy-seven of 115 men in Phelan's unit died at Andersonville. **the Wirtz case:** Henry Wirz (1823–65), Swiss-born warden of the infamous Confederate prisoner-of-war camp in Andersonville, Georgia. After the war he was tried by court-martial and hanged on November 10, 1865. W's misspelling of his name was not uncommon: the initial reports of the trial in both the *Tribune* and the *Times* spelled it "Wertz."

Sunday 27 Tommy got up before me this morning, dressed and went away, promising to return at four o'clock. When I got up I found to my horror that my big seal ring had disappeared, and I was not able to find it in the room. I could not imagine for a moment that he would rob me, and so supposed that he had only taken it to wear until he came back at four o'clock. But I saw nothing more of him. Night came, and he had gone to Washington. ¶Went to pay my bill at the St Cloud and was charged extra for Tommy, made a row about it and packed up my duds to leave.

Monday 28 Got a dray and sent my baggage to the Lloyd House, corner of Polk and Clark, near the State street cars, where I have a nice little room, and only for $8 per week. Feel quite contented with the change. ¶Found to my great horror that my soldier boy had given me crabs, and worse than that, head lice. Found my corpus alive with vermin, and shuddered at the thought. Resorted to ample potations of anquinnin and everything else, not forgetting to use a fine toothed comb. O! horror!!

anquinnin: an idiosyncratic spelling of quinine?

Tuesday 29 Yet I love the boy. There is an indescribable something about him fascinating in the extreme. The present devotion to myself, professing the most ardent love, and still so refined and the hero of so many battles and prisons. Perhaps he did not take the ring—and he, a homeless wanderer—is not to blame for giving me the horrible vermin! I will trust him, and believe that he did not take the ring. ¶Preparations for the great opening of the Chamber of Commerce. Did not do much but look around all day.

Wednesday 30 At the Sherman House and met Fort, Getty, Collins and several others from Oswego delegates to the convention. ¶Went to the great convention, and made a report of the appearance of the crowd. It was a big thing, but has a sequel, as will soon appear. We published a full page upon it. ¶Became acquainted with Maguire of the Boston Journal, and several others. ¶Went to the grand concert at the Opera house in the evening. ¶Nothing from Tommy yet!

Fort: D. G. Fort, mayor of Oswego, spoke at the opening ceremony of the Chicago Board of Trade. **Getty:** A. B. Getty, a delegate from Oswego to the gala opening. Collins is not mentioned as an Oswego delegate in the newspaper reports. **great convention:** the inaugural ceremonies of the new Chicago Chamber of Commerce Building, which included the Chicago Board of Trade on its second floor. The building was on the southeast corner of Washington and LaSalle streets. **grand concert:** This was part of the opening celebrations. Some of the pieces performed were the *William Tell Overture* by Giacchino Rossini, the allegretto from Ludwig von Beethoven's *Eighth Symphony,* and an aria from Giuseppe Verdi's *Ernani.*

Thursday 31 For a full report of to-day's adventures see my TIMES scrap book, wherein is recorded the proceedings of a drunken party on the steamer Planet. ¶At the great banquet in the evening. The board of trade, through one Clay, insulted the reporters—18 in number—and they all left the room. The thing broke up in a disgraceful drunken row. ¶While going home in a street car, half a dozen of the vilanous board of trade men fell upon me, called me all manner of opprobrious epithets, and on my threatening to pull their noses, assaulted me.

banquet: This was the second part of the three-day festivities celebrating the new Chamber of Commerce Building. **Clay:** untraced.

SEPTEMBER

Friday 1 I barely escaped from the crowded street car with my life last evening. The cowards, would that I had had a revolver with me. ¶Went to the Union Stock yards on the B of T excursion, but carried my big cane with me. Fell in with Maguire of

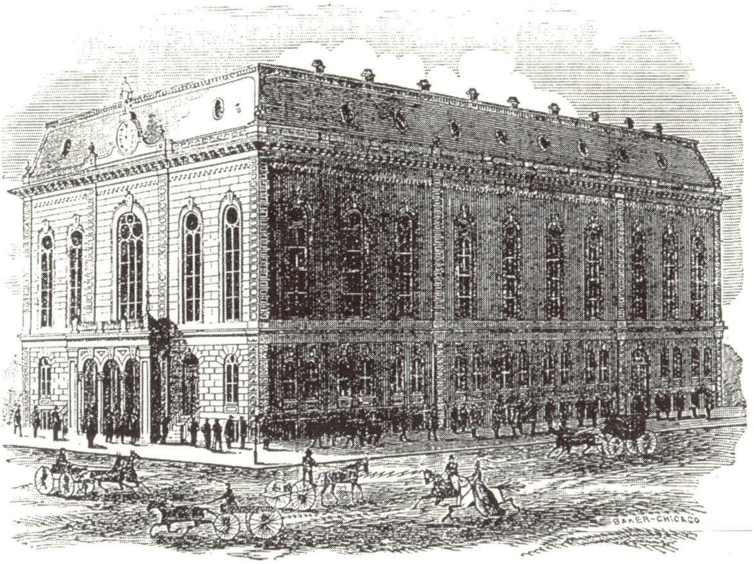

The Chamber of Commerce Building. From *Bailey's Chicago City Directory for the Year 1865–66.*

the Boston Journal. ¶Told story of the cowardly assault made upon me, and he said that he would refer to it in an editorial. ¶Went to the big ball in the evening. Fell in with the mother of dear little Johnny Pierce, and introduced myself to her.

Union Stock yards: The official opening day would be New Year's Day, 1866. **B of T:** Board of Trade. **Johnny Pierce:** a YB member W had met in the fall of 1864, when Pierce was a student in Clinton, N.Y. Pierce had returned to his home in St. Louis in December of 1864.

Saturday 2 Last night Tommy Phelan came to the door of the office, in a horrible old suit of ~~soldie~~ citizen's clothes. He says that he has been to Washington and back; that he had no place to stay but at the soldier's rest. The dear fellow! took him home with me, and love him better than ever. He declairs that he did not take the ring, and feels terribly that I should accuse him of it. The poor boy is an enigma—I cannot make him out. ¶The reporters held a meeting and drew up resolutions concerning Clay and the Board of Trade.

Sunday 3 Tommy Phelan says that he is going to Milwaukee, and that he don't know what he shall do with himself. The poor boy. O, that I could help him. ¶Nearly sick to-day from excessive labor all last week, and also from assault upon me, and the destitution of dear little Tommy, and his strange character. ¶Wrote letters to Anna, Frank Madison and B. C. Divine. ¶At the office in the evening, and wrote up this diary.

going to Milwaukee: In fact, Phelan returned to New York, where he graduated from Eastman's Commercial College, at Poughkeepsie, in December of 1865. In 1866 he went to Cuba for a year, returned to the States, married in 1868, and was living in New York City in 1870. **Frank Madison and B. C. Divine:** fellow YB members.

Monday 4 Goodsell returned yesterday, and now begins hard work. ¶Was sent alone to the state fair to do all the work there against about half a dozen men from the other papers each. Had a very hard day, and returned to the office late to write up. ¶Went over to the Sherman house, and saw Eastman of Canal [?] Cottage noteriety. He gave me a V and desired a puff. I pocketed the welcome greenback and as good luck would have it Goodsell told me to write him a puff.

state fair: The Illinois State Fair was held near Camp Douglas, west of Indiana Avenue. **Eastman:** untraced. **a V:** $5, from the roman numeral that appeared on the paper money of the time.

Tuesday 5 Of all the bores in newspaper life, a Fair of any sort is the worst; and especially a state Fair. Imagine one passing the whole day among endless rows of bovines, with the doleful prospect of spending a column upon their respective merits and owners at night. Such is the dilemma I find myself in to-day. Calculating that I could write about as much on cattle without seeing them, I spent the day in a remote corner of the presidents office, over a copy of THE TIMES.

endless rows of bovines: W grew up on a farm and from an early age loathed both farms and country life.

Wednesday 6 The State Fair. To-day it rains beautifully. The grounds are afloat—in a delightful state of prairie wet. Determined to write a dissertation on "Ankles," which I did at night. It called forth an indignant letter in THE *Journal,* from an injured countryman. ¶O! the horrors of a rainy day on the fair grounds!

O! the indescribable horrors of a fair of any sort at any time. Two more days of abject misery lie before me and its close.

"Ankles": This article did not appear in the *Times*. **countryman:** W means a man from the country, not a fellow citizen. See 9/21/65 for this usage.

Thursday 7 At an early hour I find myself again inside the hated enclosure of the fair grounds. Am doing the whole thing myself against four or five from each of the other papers, and beat them all. ¶In the evening met Joe Irwin, at the Lloyd, a young Canadian, with whom I am hereafter to have much to do, I believe. He is a stylish boy, and a perfect gentleman. He has a fine position in the bank of Montreal. He stayed with me, and we decided to know each other better.

Friday 8 At Bamford and Baldwins in the morning, and purchased several books. Met Joe, and he went to the fair with me, in consequence of which the dreary afternoon passed off more pleasantly. It is the last day, and I feel rejoiced. ¶Wrote out my report. Have had over a column of introductory every day, which I think has pleased well. ¶Dropped into Col. Wood's in the evening to see "Hamlet," which is now upon the boards there.

Bamford and Baldwins: William Bamford and Gilbert S. Baldwin ran a bookstore on the south side of Monroe Street, between Dearborn and Clark streets. **"Hamlet":** W may have been behind in his diary since *Hamlet* was not publicly performed at Wood's until September 11. However, this play was advertised as being "in preparation", and W may have seen a rehearsal. The plays performed at Wood's this evening were the same double bill as on 7/7/65.

Saturday 9 Learn of something which makes me feel bully. Genl Grant is to be taken from Galena to-morrow on a special train, over the Illinois Central to St. Louis, stopping at Springfield, etc. I am to go with the party to St. Louis where I shall see my dear little Jack Pierce, and the Old Slave City. Can hardly contain myself for joyous emotions. Sam Medill of the *Tribune* is also to be one of the party, and Kinsley does the refreshments. Bully for us!

to-morrow: Either W miswrote or was behind in his diary, as the Grant trip did not begin until 9/12/65. **Jack Pierce:** Johnny Pierce. See 9/1/65. **Kinsley:** See 7/4/65.

Sunday 10 Spent the day in pasting up my original scraps and arranging the famous "Squatter" article in book form, preforatory to binding. ¶Joe Irwin called during the day, and is to stay with me to-night. ¶The reporters met at Binmores and organized a reportorial club, in which I have the honor to be chairman of the executive committee. We all took supper at the Masonic Restaurant, and went around town on something of a lark afterwards.

Binmores: Col. Henry Binmore, co-owner of Binmore & Nevins, stenographers and law reporters. He lived at 50 Harrison Street and was the secretary of the reportorial club. **reportorial club:** This eventually became the Bohemian Club, a social organization of Chicago reporters. **Masonic Restaurant:** In the Masonic Temple, on the east side of Dearborn between Washington and Randolph streets.

Monday 11 The long anticipated day has at length arrived. As usual with Goodsell, he crowds me for matter up to the very moment of going, when I have everything to do to get ready. ¶Purchased a Small traveling satchel, shirt and suspenders for $11, and made other preparations. ¶The train starts. Everything on board is merry. Cigars and wine are plenty and Sam and I are luxuriating on the very fat of the land. Arrive at Galena where a ball for the Genl is in progress. Fell in love with a little beauty & got the mitten. D–d poor bed.

got the mitten: was refused as a lover.

Tuesday 12 Up early without having slept a wink. Dressed as well as Galena accomodations will enable me to, and the train is off. Kinsley provides breakfast for those who were starved at the De Soto. ¶Averdupois, alias Judge Ayre, a good Copperhead, gave me a sawbuck, in view of my being a TIMES man. Judge you are a brick. Fear you will never see the X again. ¶Arrive at Springfield. Sam & I have a good room at the St. Nicholas. Went and telegraphed 4,000 [words]. Visited the governor's mansion in the evening. D–d hot night, and millions of mosquitoes.

Judge Ayre: untraced. **sawbuck, . . . X:** $10 bill.

Wednesday 13 Got up at 6 o'clock, and Sam, Pratt and myself took a livery team and drove to Oak Ridge Cemetery, to visit the grave of Lincoln. The stillness of the early morning was about the place, and we felt it so visibly as we gazed on the coffin of the great dead. Returning to breakfast we were invited to join Genl Grant's party who were about to go there; did so, and saw the general at the tomb. ¶The train sped on its way to St. Louis, which city was reached in the afternoon. We were conveyed to the Lindell in carriages, Sam and I took a bath, and then went to report.

Sam: Sam Medill of the *Tribune*. **Pratt:** From the context, this might appear to be another newspaperman, but I have been unable to find anyone by that name working for a Chicago paper at the time. There was, however, Cyrus N. Pratt, agent for the Chicago and St. Louis Railroad, who may have been traveling on Grant's train to St. Louis.

Thursday 14 Called for Johnny Pierce last night, and found the dear little fellow. He reminds me of days that are flown, yet live vividly in memory. He lives in a palatial residence; and the family treated me very kindly. Jack took me to the Lacade races, and bought me a magnificent seal ring for $28. In the evening he Sam and I left our valuables at the Lindell office and went on a lark, with poor success. Johnny stayed with me at the Lindell. The special trains starts for Chicago at 8 o'clock to-morrow morning, with the English railway men on board.

English railway men: A visiting group of English entrepreneurs, including Sir Samuel Morton Peto (1809–89), a prominent railway contractor and politician. Sir Samuel published *The Resources and Prospects of America, Ascertained during a Visit to the States* shortly after this trip. W would later quote Peto's praise of the lake tunnel in his pamphlet.

Friday 15 O! the evils of boot blacks! Sent down my boots to be blacked, and could not get them this morning. Rang and sent for them repeatedly. Started down stairs in my stocking feet and met boy coming up with them. Found to my utter dismay that the party had gone, Medill and all, and I was left behind. Rushed to the ferry, but the train had gone. Returned to the Lindell in disgust, and ate breakfast. Found my way into an old bookstore and bought several old works. Started for Chicago at 3 o'c on the regular train in a sleeping car.

September 1865

Saturday 16 Was pulled out of my bunk at four o'clock this morning to walk around a freight train that had busted up on the track. Took another bunk and went to bed. Arrived in Chicago at noon, weary and fatigued. ¶Found a revolution had taken place in the office. Goodsell was in New York, and Chas Aug had been discharged, while Philip was lording it at a great rate. ¶Went out to the Union Stock Yards with the Englishmen, and wrote up the journey. At the banquet at Tremont in evening.

Tremont: See 6/9/65.

Sunday 17 A very hot and very dull Sunday. Down to the office a few moments in the forenoon, and then pasted scrap book, wrote letters, and slept. ¶It turns out that Johnson the fellow who passed himself off on Genl Grants train as a correspondent of the N. Y. Herald has stolen $7,500 worth of diamonds in St. Louis, and is now in jail. He was a precious rogue. I told Sam Medill that he was an imposter from the first. ¶Reported meeting at Bryan hall in the evening.

Bryan hall: On the east side of Clark Street, between Washington and Randolph. Built in 1860, it was the third largest auditorium in Chicago, seating 1,100, and had its own kitchen facilities for catering the fairs, balls, concerts, and other social events that were held there.

Monday 18 Went with the English party in carriages around the city, to the elevators, the University, the grave of Douglas, the Tunnel, etc. Wrote up a long article on them; and dined with them at the Tremont. ¶"The Official Report of the Formal Inauguration of the Clam and Bull Pant Bourse of Skunk-ville," is just issued, and a rich thing it is in more ways than one. As showing up the late doings of the board of trade, it could not possibly be equalled. ¶At theatre in evening.

Elevators: Between a dozen and fifteen grain elevators were located along the Chicago River and its South Branch and were the largest and tallest buildings in the city at the time, affording a grand view of both the city and the surrounding countryside. **University:** This first incarnation of the University of Chicago opened in 1859 and was near the lake on land donated by the late Senator Douglas, just southeast of Camp Douglas, between 34th and 35th streets and Cottage Grove. **grave of Douglas:** Stephen A. Douglas (1813–61) was the Vermont-born Democratic congressman from Illinois. Douglas was elected to the U.S. House of Representatives in 1843 and then to the Senate in 1847. He owned a considerable amount of real estate in Chicago, some of which he left to public institutions. The current monument at 35th Street, east of Cottage Grove, was not erected until 1881. **"The Official Report . . .":** From the title, it sounds like a printed satire on the Board of Trade. Alas, there is no record of this publication in *Check List of Chicago Ante-Fire Imprints.* **theatre:** W's choices were *Sybilla; or, Step by Step* by J. Palgrave Simpson (1807–87) and *Betsy Baker* by John M. Morton (1811–91) at Col. Wood's, or *Hamlet,* starring Lawrence P. Barrett (1838–91) at the McVicker's.

Tuesday 19 Intended to start for the Michigan state fair at Adrian this morning but as I did not awake until 7 o'clock, thought I would not go on the 6 o'clock train. ¶Passed away the day as well as possible, and departed for Adrian at 6 o'clock. Took a sleeping car and turned in, but did not sleep at all. The night was terribly cold. Arrived at Adrian at 3 o'clock in the morning and was obliged to pay $13.50 in advance for a room during the fair before I could go to bed.

Wednesday 20 Up this morning—no towel—no breakfast fit to eat. Declared to the landlord I would stop there no longer, and got my contract for a room annuled. Called at the *Watchtower* office and saw Larwill and Applegate of so many Rome memories. It is surprising what a change of time has wrought. Both are now at work on an Abolition paper & I on a Copperhead. Strange metamorphosis. ¶Went to the fair, and wrote and telegraphed my report. Stayed with Applegate.

***Watchtower*:** probably a newspaper in Adrian, Mich. **Larwill and Applegate:** friends from Rome, N.Y., where W was a typesetter, printer, and reporter for the *Roman Citizen* in 1863. W does not mention either in his diary from that period.

Thursday 21 At the fair, of which I have had quite enough and more too. Made up my mind that I might as well make something out of it, and tapped an old fellow for $3.00 for a puff. ¶Worked on cattle for Applegate. ¶Telegraphed about three quarters of a column to THE TIMES. ¶O! the horrors of stopping in a country town filled to overflowing with countrymen. It is absolutely killing; but for Applegate I could never survive.

Friday 22 On the fair grounds in the morning. Was very successful in my money scheme. Tapped three fellows for $5.00 each, for puffs, which I shall wring into my report. I find that the other fellows are doing the same thing. ¶Bid a final adieu to the grounds intending to take the 6 o'clock train for Chicago. Missed it, and telegraphed a long report. ¶Did not go to bed at night, but set up for the train at the depot. It did not come until four o'clock. Suffered terribly.

Saturday 23 The morning breaks and finds me perfectly exhausted, merely existing in a crowded car, filled to suffocation with soldiers. Never suffered more intense pain in my life. Did not arrive at Chicago until 1 o'clock, and then I was covered with dust from head to foot. At the office and find that another fair is in store for me next week. ¶Purchased a splendid saratoga trunk for $23, packed my duds and moved to No. 55, 4th Av. where Joe Irwin and I have rented a room.

saratoga trunk: a very large traveling trunk. **4th Av.:** a street between Dearborn and Clark, running from Adams to 14th Street. It is not shown on Edwards' 1866–67 map of downtown Chicago but can be found on other contemporary maps of the city. Federal Street is a vestige of this prefire street.

Sunday 24 Like my new quarters bully, and Joe is a fine companion. Unpacked my books, arranged things, etc. Went down to Kinsleys and breakfasted D. H. on dry toast and coffee. ¶Felt very sick all day. Took a dose of pills, and slept all the afternoon. ¶Recd. a letter from Geo. Best, saying that he was coming to Chicago to find a situation. Poor fellow. He knows not the difficulties he will meet with. Also received a letter from Geneva with Y.B. certificates to sign. Answered them.

D. H.: short for dead head (see 4/3/66). W frequently gained free admission to the theater and other events as a reporter, and used this popular term, "dead head," meaning someone who did not have to pay to get in. **Geo. Best:** a fraternity brother from Utica, N.Y. See 12/24/65.

Monday 25 [F]ate will have it that I must spend another week in a country town, "doing" a state fair. If accustomed to supplication, I could pray for a deliverance. But there is no other way.

¶Got ready to go this afternoon, but balmy Philip informed me that the old man wanted to see me, and so I was obliged to lay over. ¶Saw the old man, and got instructions in regard to reporting a convention.

old man: Wilbur F. Storey.

Tuesday 26 Started for Janesville, Wis, on the morning train. A ride of six hours brought me there. I found it to be a very pretty little city, but its hotels all crowded. Through a kindness of D. T. Ames of Syracuse, N.Y. I got a room with him. ¶Wrote a letter to THE TIMES, and sent by Express, giving a full description of the grounds before I saw them. it afterwards proved to be correct.

D. T. Ames: This was probably Daniel T. Ames, principal of Ames' National Business College of Syracuse, N. Y. Ames later became a prominent teacher, author, and publisher of penmanship in New York City.

Wednesday 27 Over to the fair grounds this morning, and made enough notes for a dispatch. Bled a sorghum man of $5 for a notice. ¶The Anti-Doolittle negro Sufferage convention came off in the afternoon and evening. Conally of the *Tribune* attempted to play roots upon me in regard to telegraphing, but he did not succeed. Got my entire dispatch through. ¶Went to bed very late, quite exhausted with my labors.

sorghum man: E. W. Skinner was the sorghum man (sugar manufacturer), and he did get a paragraph in W's report of the fair printed on 9/29/65. **Sufferage convention:** The Wisconsin Radical Convention. James Doolittle (1815–97) was a Republican senator from Wisconsin (1857–69) who supported the readmission of the rebel states to the union. **Conally:** J. H. Connelly, a reporter for the *Tribune*. In 1866 he would become its local editor. **play roots:** to trick or deceive.

Thursday 28 Over to the fair grounds this morning, from the Hyatt house, and took a few notes. Bled another exhibitor for $5, and then returned to the Hyatt to write my dispatches. ¶Wrote a lengthy letter on the convention, and also one on the fair. ¶Dropped into a bookstore and found a quarto edition of Hood, which I gobbled up and purchased for three dollars. ¶Went bumming with Janesville boys in the evening.

Hood: Thomas Hood (1799–1845), a humorous British poet.

Friday 29 After a pretty gay and festive time last night went home with a Janesville boy, and had a good time. Over to the fair and took notes. Ames presented me with a beautiful edition of Tennyson 2 Vols. Purchased 2 Vols of De Foe. ¶Attended a banquet to General Sherman at the Hyatt house in the evening. Reported his speech, etc. He also spoke at the fair in the morning, which I got Buckley to report. ¶Left Janesville on the 12 o'-clock train for Chicago.

Tennyson: Alfred, Lord Tennyson (1809–92). Ames possibly gave W the 1842 or 1845 two-volume London edition of Tennyson's *Poems*. **De Foe:** Daniel Defoe (1660–1731). There is not enough information to speculate which two-volume edition of Defoe W purchased. **Buckley:** George Buckley, a law-court reporter and stenographer.

Saturday 30 Arrived at Chicago about five o'clock this morning. Went to bed and slept until nearly noon, and then went to "Sharp Corners" for dinner. Settled up with the office, and made a nice thing out of the fair. ¶Brought home with me a large box of grapes "for the office." The office never eats grapes. ¶Wrote an article on Janesville, and did considerable other work. Expect to go to Indiana next week.

"Sharp Corners": The Sharp Corner Restaurant was on the southwest corner of Lasalle and Randolph streets.

OCTOBER

Sunday 1 Slept very late and then up and went to breakfast at Sharp Corners. ¶Returned to room—Joe being on his weekly visit to Desplaines—and regaled myself upon those delicious grapes. Pasted up my scrap book, read some, wrote letters, etc. ¶In the evening got hold of a shooting affray, and wrote a terrible rough article upon Capt. Hyman. As Philip would not let it go in, went to see Goodsel and he ordered it printed.

Capt. Hyman: According to W's article, the captain was a "gambler and fancy man."

Monday 2 Goodsel is greatly frightened about the article on Hyman; having been assaulted once, he has no idea of being again. He insist that I ought to carry a revolver. Therefore I purchased a "Derringer" for $12, silver mounted, and a very snotty weapon. Tried it, and it shoots bully. Now, woe to the man that molests Jack Wing. ¶Took the 10 o'clock train for Fort Wayne. Went to bed in a cosy bunk, and so far as heard from, slept well.

Snotty: nasty.

Tuesday 3 The darkey awoke me this morning about five o'clock with the cry of Fort Wayne. I arose and a colder morning never existed. Took a bus and went to the Aveline house, where everything was full and more too. Meeting Col. Dennis, of the State Board, he provides Corbett of the prairie farmer and myself with a room. ¶Went over to the fair grounds, and returning to the Aveline wrote out a very full description of them and sent by express.

Col. Dennis: untraced. **Corbett:** W. W. Corbett was coeditor of *The Prairie Farmer,* a Chicago newspaper founded in 1841.

Wednesday 4 To my great dissappointment THE TIMES appears this morning without my dispatches, all owing to the trip out to Nelson's last evening, where the shy females were met and nobody introduced. ¶On the grounds all the forenoon and bled several exhibitors of V's and X's. ¶Saw a boy with whom I fell in love, and chased him up. Found him and got him all right. Engaged a bed and he and I retired. He is a bully fellow, but got up in the night and dug.

V's and X's: $5 and $10 bills. **dug:** departed.

Thursday 5 Johnny Maier, my *enamorata* of last night, is a character in truth. Soon after he got up "to get a drink of water," I followed, and found him playing billiards and going on a big bum. Went to-bed at the Aveline, forfieting my $2. ¶THE TIMES this morning contains over two columns of fair report. ¶Around on the grounds nearly all day. Made some big strikes on puffs, and think I shall go home quite rich.

bum: a spree, outing. **forfieting my $2:** what W paid for a room he engaged to spend the night with Johnny Maier in a hotel other than the Aveline, since W was sharing a room there.

Friday 6 Settled up my bill at the Aveline and went to Senator Hoaglands on an invitation from him, found everything splendid, and regret that I had not gone there first. ¶A busy day with me. Sent off very lengthy dispatches, and took considerable money. At night found that I was $57 in, besides paying my hotel bill. Left home with $13. ¶Reported a copperhead speech in the evening, and sent it by telegraph.

Senator Hoagland: Pliney Hoagland (b. 1810), elected to the Indiana Senate in 1862.

Saturday 7 Up at six o'clock, bid goodbye to the hospitable Hoaglands, and was *en route* for Chicago. My sojourn in Fort Wayne has been altogether a pleasant and *profitable* one. ¶Reached home at 1 o'c and on setting up my account at the office found that I was in possession of $100. Saved $65 to pay for my clothes, deposited $20, and purchased $10 worth of books. ¶Recd letters from home and Geneva.

my clothes: W's disbursement of his earnings reflects a certain vanity on his part—65 percent went toward his wardrobe. In many of his diaries, he records spending much of his income on clothing, shoes, and jewelry. See, for example, 8/12/65.

Sunday 8 Joe—my room chum—is again on his Des-plaines mission. We are quite as great strangers as if we did not room to-gether. Slept very late, then up, dressed and went to barbers, afterwards to dinner at Sharp Corners. ¶Pasted up my scrap book wrote letters and diary, which occupied the entire afternoon. ¶Do not like this style of living. It's far more expensive and d—d inconvenient. But there is no other way.

Monday 9 Yes, there is another way to live, and I will try it. Began searching for a room, but without success. Determined however to secure one at all hazards. ¶Assumed my usual routine of duty in the office, but am in eager expectation of having the position of Asst City Ed again, as the "Rose" is in his usual bad odor, and rumor says that he will soon be discharged. ¶At English Opera in the evening.

the "Rose": assistant city editor, Philip. **English Opera:** They performed *Fra Diavolo* by Daniel Auber.

Tuesday 10 Inaugurated the day by writing "Gossip for Gentlemen," wherein I described and published to the world my new suit of clothes, that is to be; and said many other fine things about style. Also wrote an article upon "Our Post-office." ¶At McVicker's in the evening, and saw for the first time *"Arra na Pogue,"* the famous Irish drama. ¶Have settled into the routine of office reporting again, after my four weeks abroad.

"Arra na Pogue": *Arrah na Pogue* (first performed in England in 1864), by the Irish-born American playwright and actor Dion Boucicault (1820/22?–90), was one of the most popular American plays in the late nineteenth century (it introduced the song "The Wearing of the Green"). W saw the play again in Detroit on 3/31/66. Boucicault's *London Assurance* (first performed in 1841) was revived on Broadway in 1997.

Wednesday 11 Opened the labors of the day by penning an article on the over-sprinkling of the streets—rich, rare and racy. ¶Rock and I visit the coal yards for the purpose of ascertaining facts concerning the prices of coal. Returned and wrote an article "Subjects for Charity," which is a big burlesque upon the coal dealers, and one which will create no little excitement. ¶Got my new suit of clothes at Stevenson's, for $65. They do not suit me as well as I expected.

Rock: James L. Rock, a fellow reporter on the *Times*. **Stevenson's:** John Stevenson, draper and tailor in the Tremont House.

Thursday 12 The burlesque on the coal men has got up a hell of a row among them, as I expected. H.B.C. has also seen fit to avow his royal disgust at its appearance. But better and wiser than he affirm that it is "just the thing." ¶Got off nearly scot free to-day, so far as work is concerned. Did but very little. ¶Found a room in the new block on La Salle St. opposite the Court House, which I engage for $11 per month, and set myself about furnishing it.

H.B.C.: Henry B. Chandler, business manager of the *Times*. See 8/7/65. **block:** a common term for a building. **opposite the Court House:** W's room was actually two blocks north of the Court House on LaSalle, between Lake and South Water streets. See 10/18/65 and 1/24/66.

Friday 13 My room is a little gem in its way. The main one is 18 x 18 feet, and it has an alcove for a bed, and a commodious closet. Hired a "nig" to clean it, and went about looking for furniture. My $100 will go but a small way, but I must use it to the very *best* advantage. ¶Ordered a carpet at Palmers for 95 cents per yard, which is to be down on Monday. Am all anxiety concerning it. ¶Done very little work at the office. Only wrote a few items.

Saturday 14 Up early and went to Butters auction store, where was a set of furniture that I wanted to bid on. After waiting until nearly noon, got a chance to do so, and it was struck down to me for $50. It is a pretty white wood set of 10 pieces, and will set off my room amazingly. It cost me another dollar to get it into my room. Also bought springbed for $7, and a pair of pillows for $6. ¶Reported a race at the driving park in the afternoon. Suffered much with the cold.

Butters: auction house on the southeast corner of Dearborn and Washington streets.

Sunday 15 My last Sunday at Mammy Mills, I hope. Slept until 6 1/2, and then got up, and the morning was frightfully cold, and went to the Church of the Holy family, without breakfast, and tended to the reporting of the Consecration of the new Altar. It was a grand affair. Did not get through until about 1 o'clock at night. Had some difficulty with short hand man, etc. Wrote a good share of the report myself. Intended to present a bill for my extra services.

Church of the Holy family: Still located at Twelfth (Roosevelt Road) and May streets. The consecration of the altar in the Church of the Holy Family took place at 9:30 A.M. and was accompanied by a full orchestra and chorus. General admission was $1, and reserved seating was $2.
short hand man: W must have tried to dictate his story. See 9/29/65 and 11/30/65 for other instances of using stenographers in reporting the news.

Monday 16 Expected to get into my room to-day, but the carpet man dissapointed me about covering the floor, and had to give it up. Looking around and pricing furniture considerable. My $100 is gone, and I have not got half what I need. ¶Passed the entire day in a very uneasy state of mind. ¶In the evening an immense fire occured, which I wrote up myself. ¶Philip, the

Church of the Holy Family. From James W. Sheahan's *Chicago Illustrated* (1866).

Rose, was discharged this p.m. and Goodsell put me in the place I should have had long before—assistant city editor.

Tuesday 17 Found my carpet down this morning, and like it well. Put up my bed, arranged the room, purchased bedding, etc. Moved down my trunk from Mother Mills, and bid farewell to Cannuck Joe, and to 5th Avenue. My room is a perfect little gem, and suits me bully. ¶Bear my new office honors meekly and perform my work well. Have charge of several reporters, and all of the evening copy. ¶Wrote a statistical article upon the Coal Question.

Cannuck Joe: See 9/7/65. **5th Avenue:** The room was on 4th Avenue according to W's entry of 9/23/65.

Wednesday 18 Am now comfortably settled in no 67 Miller & Tey's block. Well well pleased with it, but penniless, let me recapitulate what it has already costs:

October 1865

Carpet ———	$28.80
Furniture set —	50.00
Mattress———	8.50
Pillows———	6.00
" cases———	2.00
Pair Sheets———	7.50
" Blankets———	5.50
Crockery———	2.75
Lamp———	1.25
Cleaning———	1.00
Total	$113.30

When I am fully "fixed up" this sum will be doubled and more too.

Miller & Tey's block: W has miswritten Tey's for Tyler's. See 1/24/66 where he also gives his room number as 20. Tyler's Block was a single building with entrances at 15, 17, 19, and 21 LaSalle Street, on the east side of the street between Lake and South Water streets (now Wacker Drive at that intersection).

Thursday 19 The ~~annul~~ solar eclipse of the sun occurred this morning being at its zenith at 9 1/2 o'clock. Wrote a somewhat lengthy and gossipy article upon it. ¶Up very late, waiting for Darling to arrive with the Boston Lancers. The Old Man came down and we had quite a little chat. He was very communicative. Does it augur well for me? ¶The expected train arrived very late, and I managed to get in a few paragraphs, so that we had the longest report in the city.

Darling: a *Times* reporter. **Boston Lancers:** a touring military drill group of Zouaves, who performed at Crosby's Opera House.

Friday 20 Spent the forenoon in taking charge of the reporters at the reception of the Boston lancers. Wrote up an introduction to the report. ¶At the banquet given to them at Bryan Hall in the evening. Darling got tight, neglected his work, etc. Up late and had in a splendid report. ¶Met Joe Lathrop of Oswego memories, at the Sherman House. Went with him to the Opera, and he then went to bed. I rejoice that he finds me as he does. It is good to my soul.

Opera: The English Opera Company was performing *The Rose of Castille*

Tyler's Block. Looking east on Lake Street. Tyler's Block is the first building to the left of the corner. From James W. Sheahan's *Chicago Illustrated* (1866).

by Michael William Balfe (1808–70), with a libretto by A. G. Harris (1825–73) and E. Falcon.

Saturday 21 This morning Darling the defaulted was dismissed preemptorily, as he deserved. ¶Purchased an over coat of Clancy, pawn broker on Randolph st. It is a bully, nobly coat, and I got it for $30, about half what it cost. ¶Made my first acquaintance with Rabelais' Works, which Chisholm just bought. Must have a copy of them at once. ¶Dropped into the Zouaves and Lancer exhibition at the Opera House. Retired at 2 1/2.

Rabelais' Works: François Rabelais (c. 1494–c. 1553). A lifelong passion begins here; in a photograph of W taken around 1915, he is holding a hefty tome boldly labeled "Rabelais."

Sunday 22 First Sunday in my room passed quite pleasantly, although a fire would have added immeasurable to its enchantment. ¶Wrote several letters, pasted up my scrap book and passed away the whole day. ¶Considerable work at the office in

October 1865

the evening. Did not get to bed much earlier than on week-day nights. ¶Thought much of home, and the approaching convention at Utica. My short funds preclude the hope of going.

convention: an Upsilon Beta convention.

Monday 23 I greatly fear that this veracious chronicle of my daily life will be found stale and insipid, even to myself. Sure it is, that I fail to infuse into it any of the *current* of my existence. When it drops behind a week, as at this writing, it is only by means of the hardest pull that I am able to bring it up. ¶Besides revising and editing all the copy in the evening, I went to and wrote up the catholic orphan's fair, in a manner afterwards complimented by the manager.

Tuesday 24 After discharging my other multifarious duties in the evening, I investigated and wrote up nearly a column entitled "An Appalling Leap," ect. Went and saw the female who jumpted 40 feet for her "dear Isaac" but did not feel like condoling with her much. ¶My room is extremely h[illegible], and I rejoice at the good fare of the sharp corners, and am glad. But I am d—d hard up, and am growing more so every day.

Wednesday 25 The responsibility connected with my present "parish" is by no means to be laughed at. It is far more responsible that [miswritten for "than"] city editor, for in fact I do nearly everything in that department. ¶In the evening was very much crowded by work. Everything to do and take the responsibility of; and not a reporter in the office competent to make a respectable item. ¶Recd a bully letter from Carpenter of the Alpha chapter Upsilon Beta.

Thursday 26 Goodsell and I took the Republican County convention at the court house. Our first move was to astonish the Republican reporters by vaulting into the secretary's place, and singing upon [a] table, etc. I appropriateing an inverted saw dust spittoon as my seat. Made a rich and racy report of the proceedings. ¶Full change of everything at the office in the evening. Did not get away until after midnight, and then went to my batchelors room on LaSalle St.

convention: This was a nominating convention for the county elections to be held on November 7.

Friday 27 A long letter from Deck Pomeroy, my old Roman friend. He discovers at some length concerning "Fan," "the only girl I ever loved" and the only one I fear that will ever love me, aside from Anna. The letter brings me back to the days of yore—to those sad yet O how happy days spent in Rome, when the laurels of a printers devil graced my brows, and I lived luxuriously upon the salary of $2 per week. O! Halcyon days—flown—but not forgotten.

Deck Pomeroy: This is Dick Pomeroy, mentioned below on 10/30/65. Another instance of W's phonetic spelling, or perhaps the use of a nickname. **Fan:** Fan Churchill of Rome, N.Y., was W's girlfriend for a few months in 1863. **$2 per week:** W's income was more than $2 a week, as he was paid according to how much type he set and averaged about $5 a week.

Saturday 28 Several political meetings in the evening—the nomination of a new ticket etc. Labored terribly upon it, and got it all up stairs early, and in good shape. The old man came at midnight, sadly out of sorts, and could not tell how it went. He sent after me but I was not to be found, or rather my room was not. He swore and raised hell generally. The paper went to press with the report dumped in, in the most outrageous style possible. The old man enraged!

political meetings: See 10/26/65.

Sunday 29 At the office this morning to receive the condemnation of old Man Story, who is perfectly enraged because he made a bull in making up the local last night. It appears that he sent to my room for me, that no one knew where I held forth, and that he swore tempestously. But no good, I could not be found, and so Jack Wing slept on perfectly unconcious of the damning he was getting. ¶An exceedingly dull day. Spent most of it at the office.

Monday 30 This morning the bollaxed report came out all straight, having been fixed over and patched up. The old man says nothing, in the day time, but in the evening I had occasion to refer some resolutions to him. He snaped me up by saying that "he did'nt run the Local" and by foaming immensely at the mouth. ¶Wrote a little, and managed to pass away the time as easily as possible. Recd a letter from Dick Pomeroy, which determined me to go to the Convention on the 14th at Utica.

He snaped me up: made an angry retort or remark. (W has misspelled *snapped*).

Tuesday 31 An exceedingly hard evenings work. Wrote an article upon the registry of voters, which was statistical in its character, and withal a pretty good thing. Water was struck at the Artesian well, and I prepared and sent up a long outside article upon it. ¶Making arrangements for my eastern trip as rapidly as possible. All that is lacking now is about $50 in money, which I fear will not be forthcoming. Am d—d hard up—never more so!

NOVEMBER

Wednesday 1 The redoubtable and impertinent Charles, brother of "he who sits upon the throne of authority" is instituting a crusade against me for the purpose of causing my ejectment from my present position and his promotion. He uses all kinds of impertinence, and he's like a professor. Will he succeed? Time alone can solve the riddle. The typos of the 'Tiser leadered by read-haired Randolph succeeded, but they were backed by the meanest of god's mean men. No. I defy him!

Charles: W's nemesis, Charles Aug and not Charles Godsell who, as local editor, could have simply fired W. **typos:** typesetters. **'Tiser:** See 6/7/65.

Thursday 2 At the office early and wrote a lengthy article upon the Great American traveller, Genl Pratt: in which I indulged in some pregnant hits at the munificent gentlemen of the Chicago Corporation and Board of Trade. ¶My batchelors quarters in the new block on LaSalle Street are my home, *all mine*! But it is cold there yet—no stove—and not enough quilts on the bed. But there are better days in store for me I hope and for my room.

Genl Pratt: According to W's article, Pratt was an elderly, eccentric wanderer.

Friday 3 The Annual Convention of the Upsilon Beta occurs the 14th inst. and I am expected to be there. Fitting up my room made me hard up as hell, and I cannot imagine how I shall get there. But if it a possible thing, I will meet the dear old boys on that occassion. And, if possible, I must go home, for it is not many times more that I shall have a father and dear old mother to visit. Poverty, affliction and increasing labor through a long life, has well nigh used them. Would that I could help them.

Saturday 4 Wrote several short articles on the pending Election, and did much promiscuous loafing on a grand scale. ¶As the 14th inst—the grand re-union at Utica, draws nigh, I grow more and more uneasy, and disinclined for office duties. My whole nature is so bound up in the dear old YB society, that I can think of little else than the beloved brothers I shall meet at the convention. ¶Wrote some on my address, etc.

Sunday 5 A direful fate seems to be mine to-day. Went to the office and was told to go with the wily Chas. Aug to Dr. Clarkson's, and procure a sermon. Went. Of course "my brother" done all the talking, and when it came to copying, I did all the work. Spent the early part of the evening sending up copy, and then sat down and finished my YB address; which pleases me well. ¶Making all the arrangements possible for my trip, but am d—d hard up.

Dr. Clarkson's: The Reverend Robert H. Clarkson was the rector of St. James Episcopal Church. This church was rebuilt after the fire at its original location of Huron and Cass (now Wabash) streets.

Monday 6 Chas Aug is still on his taps, and many are the tales of persecution poured into the willing ears of my brother. But it is no use. One stands no chance whatever, and my destiny is already sealed. Yet I remember the satisfaction I once had of soundly snubbing him. ¶To-morrow is election and then on Wednesday I take my departure, on my long, O! how long, contemplated journey home, and to the YB's. ¶Wrote a string of gossip about the weather, etc.

Tuesday 7 Election day, and the soldiers ticket beaten. Charles

Aug received the entire credit of getting the returns, and got none of them. ¶A damnable boil has made its appearance on my neck, and I cannot wear a collar. Curse my bad blood! All summer, when a boil would have been a luxury, I have gone scot free, now it will spoil my entire trip. Damnation! ¶Sold my old suite of clothes for $7.00, and Stridiron advanced me my week's $25; so that I shall be able to start with about $40. Too small by five.

Election day: county election day for judges, clerk, treasurer, school commissioner, etc. **soldiers ticket:** A splinter group, from the Republican party, of soldiers and veterans, also known as "bolters." **Stridiron:** John E. Stridiron was the accountant for the *Times.*

Wednesday 8 Procured a pass over the Grand Trunk of Canada, packed my trunk, got a lunch put up D. H. at Kinsleys, put a stiff collar on my boil, and left the Garden City for the dear old Empire State. Took a bunk in a sleeping car but my neck is terrible painful. I "tried natures sweet restorer" [but it] gave me the slip entirely. ¶From all appearances it is probable that Chas Aug is to succeed me, and that on my return I shall find myself superceded. Things look damdly that way, at all events.

D. H.: dead head. Here, it must mean W got his lunch for free. See 9/24/65.

> [*W's first trip back east.* W returns to upstate New York by train, arriving in Buffalo Thursday evening. After visiting friends in Syracuse he arrives home on the eleventh, where he stays until the Upsilon Beta Convention in Utica on the fourteenth. He starts his return west on the twentieth, stopping briefly in Detroit to visit friends before heading to Chicago.]

Thursday 23 Arrived in Chicago about noon. Found my room all right, and the things in my trunk nearly so. Unpacked them and arranged my room, and then went to the TIMES office. There all is changed. Jim Chisholm has left, and as I surmised Chas. Aug has superceded me. Goodsell will not vouchsafe an explanation, but sets me to work upon an article upon the stock yards. My money is gone, I am terribly in debt, and get the cold shoulder from the office. Jack, your journey has been a costly one.

Jim Chisholm: Chisholm went to work for the *Chicago Tribune*. **stock yards:** W had first visited the Union Stock Yards on 9/1/65, but this upcoming visit would soon play an important role in W's financial well-being.

Friday 24 Attempted to get a situation at the REPUBLICAN office last night, but was bluffed by England, in a manner that I did not deserve. Where will it end. ¶Goodsell, Rock and myself rode out to the stock yards this morning, and I feel a little better in my mind. There are to be some important changes in the office, but how they will result in regard to me, I cannot surmise. ¶Went to the opera in the evening, but in my state of mind did not enjoy it much.

bluffed: dissuaded. **England:** assistant city editor of the *Republican*? On 12/1/65 and 12/21/65, he is compared to the *Times*'s assistant editor Charles Aug. **Rock:** see 10/11/65. **opera:** Gaetano Donizetti's *Elisir d'amore* and the duet act of his *La favorita* were performed at Crosby's that evening.

Saturday 25 My envelope today contains a bill, bringing me in debt to the office over $2.00. Raised a blow about it, which resulted in the office triumphing, and my being cheated out of my salary and the extra work I have done. Goodsell also got his back up. ¶Went out to the stock yards and spent the afternoon. Made a futile attempt to get a job of writing a pamphlet. Returned to town, and pawned my revolver for money to send Anna and Barry White. Wrote late on my article.

got his back up: things were getting tense at the *Times* office. On November 28, a libel suit for $25,000 was brought against W. F. Storey by Van H. Higgins, an former superior court judge. **Anna:** W had been supplying his sister's tuition and school expenses for several years. A remark in a letter he wrote to her in 1868 suggests that he may have even offered to pay her tuition to Mount Holyoke College. **Barry White:** fellow YB from whom W had borrowed money to get from New York back to Chicago.

Sunday 26 To-day—this cold November Sabbath, finds me in about the worse fix I was ever in, with little or no prospects for an extrication. Big rent and board bill stare me in the face, and I have not a solitary cent in the world. ¶But there are better days in store. I shall make an effort to-morrow to get up a pamphlet, and I may or may not suceed. ¶Worked at the office in the evening, under Chas. Aug.

Monday 27 Canvassed around as to the prospects for making something out of a pamphlet on the Stock Yards. Did not make out much. ¶Wrote upon my Stock Yard article nearly all day. Chas Aug has succeeded in getting me in ill odor with his omnipotent brother. He evidently intends to discharge me the first opportunity, or as soon as the article is finished. But we will see about that thing.

Tuesday 28 Saw Tucker of the Brigg House this morning and he says he will take 500 of the pamphlets, if I will publish them. Made up my mind to undertake it, and run the risk. Saw the railroad men, and they agree to take one hundred of the copies apiece. ¶So far I am getting along bully with it. If a number of advertisments can be secured, I think I can make it pay bully. So here goes.

Brigg House: Briggs House, a hotel on the northeast corner of Wells and Randolph streets, built by William Briggs in 1853 and sold to William F. Tucker and J. H. Silsby in 1858. **Saw the railroad men:** Curiously, there are no railroad advertisements in either edition of the Stock Yards pamphlet. The railroads, of course, had made the Union Stock Yards possible.

Wednesday 29 Went on an excursion to the tunnel crib in the afternoon, with a party of Bostonians and down in the tunnel and out to the extreme end with them in the evening. It was a very fine trip. Returned to the office late, and wrote up a long report of it, which seems to please everybody connected with the party. Done some more canvassing on my pamphlet, with success in a slight degree.

tunnel crib: See 7/6/65 for W's first visit to the lake tunnel.

Thursday 30 Now that I am fairly into this venture, I will carry it through, make or lose—lose, how can I—when I have nothing to lose. ¶Was put in Charge of half a score of "short hand" Irishmen, to report the St Andrews Supper this evening. Got along as well as I could with them, by working very hard myself. I felt very sanguine over my speculation. If I succeed, it will be the biggest thing on record!

DECEMBER

Friday 1 Went out to the Yards in the afternoon, and succeeded in getting information concerning the old yards, and also the cards of 4 cattle men for my pamphlet, at $25 a piece. Pretty good. ¶Got down to the office late. Everything concerning my book goes well, but the best thing I can do is to leave the office at once. ¶England sent for me and offered me a situation upon The Republican at $25 per week, which I accepted.

Saturday 2 Now that I am bound to resent the insults that have been offered me by the Goodsells, I do about as I please. Went to the Yards in afternoon, got 2 cards and $25 in advance. Put up a gas fixture and gas stove in my room. ¶Goodsell sent me to report the Train, then called me away and sent me to a fire, which I did not go to. Went to the office and got my things, and the copy on the stock yard article, left Goodsel and the old man a note saying that "He had a brother," and dug out. Fit finale after such treatment.

"He had a brother": This allusion's meaning completely escapes me.

Sunday 3 I think the city editor of THE TIMES will soon find out that he has a younger brother, if many more of his old staff leave. But he is frightfully obtuse. ¶Spent the entire day in copying the Stock Yard article. In the evening took the first 90 pages of it to the office and left it with my keys, etc. Shall put it into the hands of a good job printer in the morning, and get out the pamphlet as soon as possible. ¶This bids fair to be an important week for me.

Monday 4 Took my manuscript to Thompsons Job office and he immediately commenced work upon it. Canvassed for advertisements with the most flattering success. Made all necessary arrangements. Copied the remainder of the manuscript, and sent it to the office. Went there after letters in the evening, and Chas. Aug. made several threats about my not having finished the article. Some difficulty may come from it, but the probable success of the enterprise overbalances them.

Thompsons: Jeremiah S. Thompson's printing office was between Washington and Randoph streets, on the west side of Dearborn Street.

He was the manager of the printing department of the Religio-Philosophical Publishing Association (next door at 84 Dearborn), whose imprint W used on the Stock Yards pamphlet.

Tuesday 5 Read some of the proof upon my book, and every thing goes on well. On going to Bakers to get the engraving, I found he would not let me have it, which necessitated me going to the stock yards after another, and will put off the publication of the pamphlet. But now I am fairly in for it, come weal or woe, and I am bound to push it through at all hazards. The dissapointment on the cut makes me rather blue. Went to theatre in the evening.

to Bakers: William D. Baker's wood-engraving house was on the corner of Clark and Randolph streets, next door to Col. Wood's Theatre and Museum. **engraving:** W must have tried to borrow an existing wood engraving of a plan of the Stock Yards. See the following entries. **theatre:** W had several choices: *Belphegor: or the Bride of Birth* by Charles Webb (1834–1905) was playing at Col. Wood's. At the McVicker's were *Born to Good Luck* by Tyrone Power (1797–1841), *The Young Actress* by Dion Boucicault, songs and dances by Mrs. Florence, and *The Returned Volunteer* by an unknown author, all performed by the acting company of the husband-and-wife team of William J. Florence (1831–91) and Malvina Florence (1831–1906). Kelly & Leon's Minstrels were performing at the Academy of Music.

Wednesday 6 Went out to the Union Stock Yards at noon, and Civer promised to prepare me a diagram of the yards, and send to Thompsons office to-morrow. Rode down with Tucker, and got some encourgment as to the success of my enterprise. ¶Told England that I would help him to-morrow if he liked, and was assigned the services in the charitable institutions of the city, situated about 5 miles apart, in every direction. Read more proof upon my pamphlet. Went to Wood's in evening.

Civer: W. H. Civer, resident engineer for Union Stock Yards, was mentioned in W's pamphlet. **Tucker:** W. F. Tucker, co-owner of the Briggs House Hotel and the proprietor of the Hough House Hotel at the Union Stock Yards. **Wood's:** *Belphegor* was still playing at Col. Wood's.

Thursday 7 There are asses everywhere. Today when Civer sent my diagram to the office where the book was printing, a d—d fool sent him to the TIMES office with it. Went to see if

Rock could not get it for me. ¶Went around to the charitable institutions of the city, working for THE REPUBLICAN. My Thanksgiving was as gloomy and dull a one as I ever passed. But they are all so. To-day I am distracted when I think of the work before me, on my pamphlet, and the risk I run.

Thanksgiving: This new holiday fell on December 7th in 1865.

Friday 8 As good luck would have it, I found my diagram at Thompsons this morning. Baker promised to engrave it for me for $20 and finish it by next Tuesday. It will not do to put it upon the public without this most essential feature, so I set him to work. The printing gets along bully, and I ought to have the thing out on Wednesday next, and get settled up by saturday. Then I shall be the happiest man in America.

Saturday 9 Very little I can do now on my pamphlet, until the cut is done. Obtained a $25 Advertisement from Bryant & Stratton, and read some proof. Helped England on The REPUBLICAN, and believe that my new situation there is agoing to be a fine one in the extreme. ¶Jack Wing, you predict for yourself a pocket full of money by one week from to-night. Take good care that it does not fail. And thus I will be a lucky boy indeed.

Bryant & Stratton: see 7/19/65.

Sunday 10 Spent the day in a semi-sorrowful state of mind. The many difficulties that I have encountered this far with getting out my pamphlet loom up more prominent in the distance, as I see those yet to be meet. ¶Tomorrow I commence for good upon The Republican. I hope my sojourn in that office may be long and peaceful; and that I shall find no Chas. Aug. there. The point is always small upon which the scales turn, so in this case.

The Republican: at 93 Washington Street.

Monday 11 Luckily I found the drawing of the stock yards at Thompsons this morning and immediately put it into the hands of an engraver who promised it to me on Tuesday afternoon. Everything now seems to be working well. Canvassed my regular work upon the Republican. Am treated with the utmost cordiality and good feeling there. I trust I shall like it much.

The opening of this entry is nearly the same as that for 12/8/65, suggesting W may have fallen behind in his diary.

Tuesday 12 Spent nearly the entire day in Colburn's office, copying the list of vessels in the harbor. ¶Got my cut from the engraver and took it to Thompson's. Am to have some copies to-morrow. ¶Was obliged to ask Col Wood to pay me his $25 in advance, $20 of which I paid for the engraving. ¶I [came] back,[and] the garrulous Fenton with whom I have been boarding, at Sharp Corners, gets his back up and gives me my bill, which I pay and dig out.

Colburn's office: Theodore F. Colburn, owner of Colburn's Tugboats whose office was located along the river on the north side of South Water Street between Dearborn and Clark streets. **Fenton:** possibly Thomas Fenton, a printer for the *Chicago Evening Journal.*

Wednesday 13 Got some copies of my long looked for pamphlet on the Stock Yards this evening. They look bully; quite as well as I ever hoped them to look. Collected $25 in the evening of Belding and $25 of Bauer, and feel as though I had got a pretty good start. To-morrow will be my great day's work upon it. I must arise and get to Briggs House at 7 o'clock, to meet Tucker there, and get my pay for his copies. Retired quite elated & determined to get up.

Belding and . . . Bauer: clothier and musical instrument importer and manufacturer, respectively, both full page advertisers in both editions of *The Great Union Stock Yards of Chicago*. **Tucker:** see 12/6/65.

Thursday 14 Got up at 6 1/2 o'clock and went post haste to the Briggs House. Found Tucker there, and gave him a specimen copy of the pamphlet. he gave me a check for $125. After breakfast started collecting. Got my money of all the railroads, and of nearly all the other parties. Deposited $200 in the bank, and have got considerable to collect. Am surprised at my great success! It is better than I even hoped for. A decided streak of luck, I say, Jack! ¶Went to bed very gay in spirits.

railroads: The unspecified number of railroads each bought 100 copies of the pamphlet. See 11/28/65.

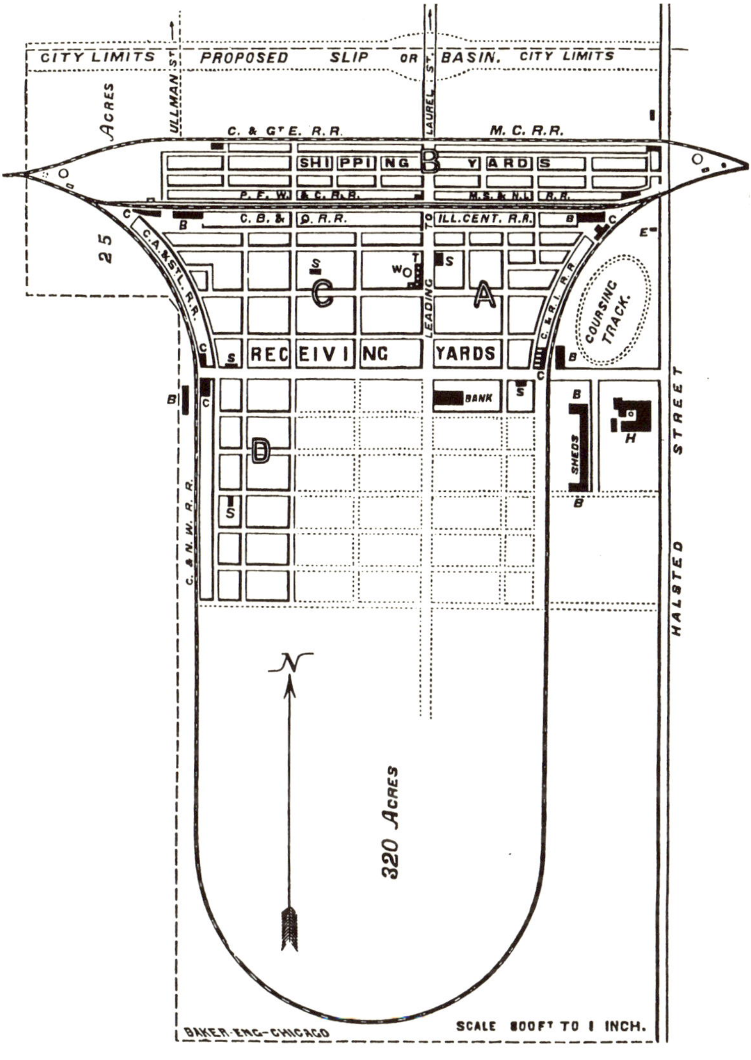

Plan of the Union Stock Yards. This is the frontispiece to W's pamphlet *The Great Union Stock Yards of Chicago*. Although there are letters on this map, there is no key and W did not refer to the letters in his text. Hough House is on the right at *H*. (78% of actual size.)

Friday 15 Got to the Jail at 9 1/2, met Connelly there and we went inside to see Corbett & Fleming, the condemned murders, to die at 2 o'clock. Witnessed the performance of Mass, and other solemn ceremonies of the Catholic Church. Stayed in the loathsome jail nearly all day, and witnessed the hanging of the two men, at 2:30. It was a terrible sight, but since the hanging of Bell, I do not mind it much. ¶Collected $50 and got a splendid sofa at Tobey's for $65.

Connelly: See 9/27/65. **Corbett & Fleming:** William Corbett and Patrick Fleming were sentenced to death on November 25, 1865, for the murder of Patrick Maloney the previous November. Both W and Connelly witnessed the execution. **Bell:** William Bell. See 6/29/65 and 7/5/65. **Tobey's:** Chas. Tobey & Bro. took a full-page ad in the first printing of the pamphlet but had none in the second.

Saturday 16 Got up early and went to the stock yards. Had no difficulty in collecting all my bills, and came back with $110 as my morning's work. Deposited $150 in the Illinois State Savings Bank, making my deposite there $350.00, the largest sum I ever possessed. Bully for me! ¶Reported details of the great Lake street fire, and went to a meeting in the evening. Everything works bully. Drew my salary from the time I commenced on the REPUBLICAN.

Sunday 17 Pecuniarily, this is the happiest Sunday of my life, thus far. One week ago I would have given much to have known exactly how I should come out of my successful enterprise, as it has now proved. From actual figures I have made over $500—$350 of it in clean greenbacks. ¶Wrote several letters, one sending my new engraved YB cards to Walnut Hill boys, and also to the Utica boys. ¶Got Dr. Ryder's sermon in the evening.

clean greenbacks: cash, as opposed to payment in goods. **Dr. Ryder's sermon:** The Reverend William H. Ryder (b. 1822) was pastor of St. Paul's Universalist Church, located at Wabash and Van Buren streets.

Monday 18 On police and fires, which of all kinds of reportorial work I most supremely detest. ¶Billy Bissel whom I met in Detroit, came to the office. He agreed to stay over night. Went to the opera, and then to my room. Billy is a brick—a *roue*! How the night passed, let memory only know. It was hapiness, bliss. He is my beau-ideal, and answers well in the place of dear Dick [Pomeroy], or Barry [White]. Do not know what time we closed our weary eyes.

opera: Charles Gounod's *Faust* was playing at Crosby's Opera House. ***roue***: I'm not sure what W means in this sudden outburst of French. Clearly an approving usage and not the dictionary definition of a "debaucher or rake" or "man devoted to sensual pleasure." **Dick . . . Barry:** fellow YB fraternity brothers from upstate New York.

Tuesday 19 Billy went away before breakfast, and with him went many joys. I must go to Detroit soon, and enjoy another season with the Hanky boy of the Auditor's office. ¶Police and Fires—the latter to excess. It seems as if the whole d—d town would burn down, while I have the [reporting of] fires on my hands. But there is no help for it. Hell-wards in the evening, searching after "items." The last named commodity was d—d scarce.

Hanky boy: probably W's variant of *hanky-spanky*, a dashing, stylish person. Here it refers to Billy Bissell. **Hell-wards:** perhaps a pun, towards Hell, i.e., over to city wards noted for crime and vice.

Wednesday 20 The call for another edition of my pamphlet seems to be called for. If they will order enough to make it pay, I will print a large edition of them. I think they will come to their milk. ¶Am actually growing despeptic since I went to the Briggs. Eat I must when it is set before me, and eat I do, I assure you. ¶The regular office work, police and Fires. Everything lovely, only my boots d—d wet by the snow.

Thursday 21 An overture of curses this morning in [room] 67; played upon too tight boots, nicely shrunk by the wet snow of last evening. But I finally got inside of them and proceeded to the Briggs to breakfast, and then at the armory, where another diurnal round of misery met my eyes. ¶Dropped into the Museum a few moments in the evening. England seems fond of working me like hell; but it is more agreeable than under Chas Aug.

Museum: The last performance of the famous dramatization of *Uncle Tom's Cabin* by G. L. Aiken (1830–76) was at Col. Wood's this evening.

Friday 22 1865 is drawing hurridly to a close, & this diary—the companion of the most properous year of my life—will soon be laid away among its predecessors. Not[e] here daily marked my life in sad and happy hours that are past. ¶The usual work at the office, day and evening. Drew my $25 less $2, which the sharks retained to pay for a weekly sent to the old gentleman. Did not fancy it much but too late.

the old gentleman: W's father, Mansir Wing.

Saturday 23 Purchased a diamond pin and case at Giles Brothers for $50, which I drew from the bank. It is a perfect gem, and I propose to exchange it for a more expensive one as soon as I am able. Diamonds are my delight—diamond pins or diamond friends, in the shape of whole souled boys. ¶Recd a splendid letter from Anna, wishing me a merry Christmas. I hope hers will be such.

Sunday 24 Wrote a letter to Geo Best and Barry White, sending some of my new YB cards for the boys. ¶In the afternoon Hopkins, whom I have under obligations to as the giver of 2 spittoons for my room, came to my apartment, and we went on the West side to report a meeting. The Reporters Club was to meet at my room in the morning, but nobody came but Sam Medill and Colbert of the *Tribune*. At work in the evening.

Hopkins: Mordecai L. Hopkins, assistant editor of the *Chicago Times*. **Colbert:** Elias Colbert (1831–1921) was born in England and migrated to the U.S. and Chicago in 1857. He was a stenographer and organized the Northwestern Phonographic Institute in the city. Colbert had worked for the *Times* in 1862–63 but switched to the *Tribune*, where he became its commercial editor in 1866. He wrote a Chicago history, *Chicago. Historical and Statistical Sketch of the Garden City* (1868) and, with Everett Chamberlin, coauthored the first book published on the city after the fire, *Chicago and the Great Conflagration* (1871). He was an amateur astronomer and published in that field and taught astronomy at the University of Chicago.

Monday 25 "Christmas," but all but a merry one to me, because so far away from those I love. ¶Done about the usual office work, and loafed around town. Billy Bolshaw presented me with a box of cigars, for which I shall ever hold him in the utmost reverence. ¶At the office late in the evening as usual, and went to bed tired and dispirited, notwithstanding my diamond pin is glistening on the bureau.

Billy Bolshaw: William H. Bolshaw was the proprietor of the Matteson Saloon and Billiard Room. This mention of W's only Christmas gift is telling: in addition to his frequent vistits to Col. Wood's Theatre, he must have also been a regular at the nearby Matteson House saloon to merit such a gift from its proprietor.

Tuesday 26 Saw Col Hough at the Briggs, and he demands that I publish another edition of the Stock Yards pamphlet, and says that he will take 200 copies. This is rather encouraging; I may make some more out of the yards. Commenced to look about me, and arrange things. Called at several places, but did not meet with very good success. ¶Wrote a letter to Billy Bissell, telling him that I thought I would be in Detroit New Years.

Hough: Rosell M. Hough, colonel in the 67th Illinois regiment during the war. He and his brother Oramel were early Chicago meat packers. Rosell was the president of the Chamber of Commerce and was also superintendent of construction of the Union Stock Yards. The six-story Union Stock Yards Hotel was renamed Hough House in his honor. **another edition:** A private opening of the Union Stock Yards was held on Christmas day and, the Colonel must have distributed copies of the Stock Yard pamphlet to his guests.

Wednesday 27 Rushed around to the armory and got through as soon as possible, then canvassed on my book. ¶Dunlap of the Northwestern [Railroad] says that he will take 200 copies, which is a beginning. ¶In the evening wrote a long Christmas letter to Annie, sending her an X greenback as a holiday present, although I hardly know how to spare it. ¶Got an Indian murder sensation, and wrote it out in full at a late hour.

Dunlap: George L. Dunlap (b. 1828) was general superintendant of the Chicago and Northwestern Railroad.

Thursday 28 Am bored to the death by England, to get up statistics concerning the live stock trade. It is an immense work. ¶Fairbanks and Greenleaf say that they will take $2,000 of my pamphlets at $350. This is indeed a lift. Burling & Co will take a hundred, and so I am getting on nicely. Nothing would suit the subscriber better than to have as good luck on this as on the first edition. He'll try for it.

Fairbanks and Greenleaf: scale merchants at 226–228 East Lake Street, west of the south branch of the Chicago River. **$2,000:** Clearly

Hough House. This hotel was located on the east side of the Union Stock Yards along Halsted Street. From James W. Sheahan's *Chicago Illustrated* (1866).

W has miswritten $2,000 for 2,000. See the next entry for the size of the second edition. **Burling & Co:** Edward Burling (b. 1819) and Edward Bauman were architects who had designed both the Chicago Chamber of Commerce Building and the Hough House Hotel, among other Chicago buildings.

Friday 29 Spent every moment of my spare time out of the office working upon my Revised Edition of the Stock Yard Pamphlet. I believe it will be successful. Thompson agreed to print me 5,000 for the sum of $350 which I think is large enough. ¶The usual office task—police and fires, the most detestable of all Bohemian employment. ¶Made up my mind that I could not spend time to go to Detroit on New Years.

5,000 for the sum of $350: The forty-eight-page second edition of the pamphlet had a remarkably low unit cost of seven cents.

Saturday 30 Spent the forenoon at the Chamber of Commerce getting the yearly statistics. ¶Drawing of the Art Union prizes in the evening and I of course drew a —. ¶Got the arrangements for my pamphlet well under way; and made arrangements for some advertising, also with the *Prairie Farmer* to let them have the cut. ¶For some unaccountable reason, Hines has been discharged from the office.

Art Union: Crosby's Opera House was holding a drawing for original paintings. **drew a —:** W's graphic way of saying he drew a blank. **my pamphlet:** The text was reset, and there are twelve pages of ads in this edition, as compared with ten pages of ads in the first printing. **cut:** an illustrated ad.

Sunday 31 And so goes out this dear old year of my prosperity, to usher in one of dread uncertainty. It has been both a happy year and sad. ¶Looking after "watch meetings["] in the evening, with poor success; accompanied by my friends of Brunswick hall dedication remembrance. ¶Got home late and Charley Wright came and slept with me. ¶And 1865 has gone out—this diary is done. God prosper me in 1866!

Brunswick hall: On the southeast corner of Washington and Clark streets, it was owned by the Brunswick Billiard Company. **Charley Wright:** see 8/15/65.

[On the last page of the Memorandum section of the diary, in pencil]

1865	1892
21	1844
[18]44	48

[This is not written in the same handwriting as the diary and may be from 1892. It reflects W's year of birth and age in 1865 and 1892.]

1866 Diary: January–December

Monday 1 The New Year! Well, and I, too, am new, so far as ambition and love and great expectations go. I believe that it finds me quite as happy and far less miserable than did 1865. A bumper to the old; it was fraught with happiness and misery—good cheer to the new—may it prosper its waif, the erratic Jack. ¶Did some canvassing for advertisements for my pamphlet, and got one of the Bryant & Strattons for $40. ¶Went out to the Union Stock Yards to a dinner in the evening, and swung a 3 column report.

Bryant & Strattons: Their ad was on the back cover of the second edition of the Union Stock Yards pamphlet. **dinner:** The Union Stock Yards officially opened this day.

Tuesday 2 The Stock Yard report this morning is bully; and may save me some money in the shape of a board bill. ¶At the Armory in the morning, and also in the afternoon. ¶Spent considerable time in canvassing for advertisements, but it was of little use. Got one from the Rubber store for $15, and also one from the PRAIRIE FARMER for $35. I believe my 2d edition will be a good success. It looks now as if I could save considerable out of it. Office work in the evening.

board bill: rent. **Rubber store:** the ad for Jno. B. Ideson & Co., Rubber Goods was a half page. **Prairie Farmer:** The *Prairie Farmer* was the first full-page ad after the text.

Wednesday 3 Labored pretty snug all day, every moment I could steal out of the office work, upon my pamphlet, which is now in press. ¶In the evening went out to the Central Skating park, and was very finely treated by Young, the proprietor, who introduced me to Miss Carrie Moore, the famous Concord skater. She did me the honor to fall upon the ice, and send for me to pick her up. Spent the evening very pleasantly, and returned to the office to write up my report.

Central Skating park: This enclosed park was also known as the Wabash Rink, and had opened on the northeast corner of Wabash and Jackson streets in the winter of 1865. W refers to it as "the Rink" on 1/17/66 and after. **Young:** Caryl Young. **Miss Carrie Moore:** a professional ice-skater from New Hampshire.

Thursday 4 Got down to the Armory about 10 o'clock, and got back to the office at 11. ¶Read some proof upon my 2d edition. ¶It is singular that I do not hear from Walnut Hill, Clinton or ~~Gener~~ Atica. Not a word from any of the dear old boys in over two weeks. ¶Stole away a few moments in the evening, and went up to Central Park, but was too late to see either Young or Miss Moore. ¶My night up, and a d—d hard one too.

Walnut Hill . . . Atica: locations of YB chapters in upstate New York.

Friday 5 Oh what woe, what dark foreboding cloud is this! ¶When "the judge" payed me this morning, he attempted to make me take $10 in five cent pieces, which I objected to. He magnified the thing to the "Dr." and in consequence I am instantly decapitated, and no words will be heard in my defense. ¶Took what few things I had at the office, and left. A more desponding spirit I never carried. In the height of my prosperity, cut off from it all! ¶Spent the day in gloomy thought. My pamphlet is all I have left—if that fails me then I am truly hard up.

"the judge": Charles Anderson Dana (1819–97), editor-in-chief of the *Republican.* Dana was assistant secretary of war (1862–65) under Edwin Stanton and had been brought to Chicago in May of 1865 specifically to run the *Republican* as a moderate paper in opposition to the more conservative *Tribune.* He failed to have any effect and left the city the following May for New York, where he became editor-in-chief of the *New York Sun.* **"Dr.":** Alonzo W. Mack (1822–71), publisher of the *Republican,* was also a physician, lawyer, soldier, legislator, and journalist.

Saturday 6 In a fit of desperation I wrote a note to Goodsell last night, asking back my place on The Times. He insolently replies that "he has no employment for me." Well, it was my *denir* resort! and I am not disappointed. ¶Wrote several letters to different county papers, enquiring if they were for sale. It is my only hope. ¶Watched the progress of my pamphlet, and canvassed for it without much success. ¶Went up to the Central Skating park, in the evening, and came down with Miss Moore, the great skater.

denir: W's spelling for the French *dernier*, last.

Sunday 7 Slept over breakfast then up and went to "Long's" for a shave. Then to dinner; and then to my room (dear old room, the creation of my own hands) where I spent most of the afternoon in gloomy drowsiness; thinking of the fate in store for me. ¶At 5 o'clock, called upon Miss Carrie Moore, the skater, at her hotel. Stayed to tea, and until after 10 o'clock. I really believe the girl loves me. *Such* a time I have not had since the happy days of my early and only love—that love which is never to be again. O! disolate, disconsolate Wing!

only love: Fan Churchill, a sixteen-year-old girl W dated in Rome, N.Y., in 1863.

Monday 8 The beginning of a week of despondency. ¶Sauntered out in the forenoon in quest of another advertisement for my pamphlet, but met with ill success. The day dragged heavily upon my hands. Very cold in my room, and no where to go. O! What a miserable day. ¶Set for a large photograph at Fasatts for what he owes me. ¶Recd a letter from G. M. Stoddard, but cannot write him now. No letters from any of the offices I wrote on Saturday. "Lost in London" at Col's in evening.

Fasatts: S. M. Fassett's Photograph Gallery, on the west side of Clark between Washington and Madison streets, was an advertiser in the first edition of the Stock Yards pamphlet. **"Lost in London":** a drama by Watts Phillips (1825–74).

Tuesday 9 Recd this morning letters from several of the offices I went [for *wrote*?] to, but they are all far beyond my small means. Obtained a pass to go to Kankakee to look at the Gazette establishment. Started for there at 9:30 and arrived at midnight. Got into the most villainous hotel that I ever saw in all my travels; too filthy to live in. Spent the night in wakefulness and despondency. ¶Can I content myself in such a place now? even if I bought into a paper? I fear the stillness would eat me up bodily.

offices I went to: there is no indication in the diary that W visited any newspaper offices, but perhaps he wrote to them.

Wednesday 10 Arose to the most damnable filthy breakfast that I ever sat down to. Paid $1.00 for the torture I had endured, and sallied forth. Found THE KANKAKEE GAZETTE, and observed the establishment. My heart sank within me. If this is worth $4,000 what must the cheaper concerns be? Spent the most doleful day of my existence in this most abject settlement. Made no attempt "to get an interest." Took the first train, at 7:30 for Chicago, to enjoy for one more night the comforts of my room.

Thursday 11 A doleful day. Wandered about the streets, looking so sadly forlorn that I almost feared that I should become suicidally inclined. Got not a word of hope; or a prospect of finding something to do. ¶Called at a place where they advertised ~~with~~ for a "partner with $500 cash," etc; but on seeing the place, did not ask what the nature of that lucrative sinecure was. ¶Got a few of my long projected pamphlets (2d edition), but did not distribute any of them. To-morrow will be my big days work.

Friday 12 At work all day distributing and collecting my booklet business. Meet with first rate success thus far, and cannot fail to make at least $400 out of it, if Greenleaf does not go back on me. ¶Deposited $150 in the Illinois State saving's institution, where the rest of my Stock Yards funds are. ¶Saw "lost in London["] at Col. Woods. ¶The agent of the Travelers Ins Co. offered me a position as canvasser at $1,500 per year, and asks me to call on Monday.

Greenleaf: See 12/28/65. **"lost in London:** Either W saw this play again, or he was behind in his diary. See 1/8/66. **The agent:** John W. Clapp. **Travelers Ins Co.:** They had a full page ad in the second edition of the Stock Yards pamphlet.

Saturday 13 Resumed my collecting and succeeded well. Everyone is coming down, and I shall probably get in all that I expected. Deposited another hundred dollars in the bank. ¶Met Jack Mattoon of Oswego, in Brunswick's in the evening, with two ducks from Canada—fancy skaters, whom he pretends to run. Jack went and stayed with me, but we did not have much of a time. He was frozen to death and found fault with my "hard bed." But he does not know anything about batcheleor living.

ducks: slang for a chaps, fellows, or persons.

Sunday 14 Went out to the "Central" with Jack Mattoon and the Meagher boys, and came back and dined with them at the Sherman. ¶In the evening we held high carnival in the parlor, and the time passed very pleasantly. They are a good lot of boys. ¶To-morrow begins a week of doubts and fears. My plan is to accept the position offered by the Insurance Co., and then during the week go to Monmouth, and look at the "Review" office.

Meagher boys: the Canadian "ducks" mentioned in the previous entry.

Monday 15 The Travelers Insurance Company still desires my services. Made an arrangement with them to commence canvassing next monday, for three months at $100 per month, and then for a year for $1,500, if all are pleased. It is better than a broken back. ¶The d—d bookbinder disappointed me on my pamphlets, but I made some collections and went to bed at night with $100 in pocket. ¶At Rink in the evening with Mattoon, the Meagers and Carrie Moore. Spent $2.60 at Kinsleys with Jack, and lost $1.75 playing lou at the Merchants hotel.

bookbinder: The pamphlet was side-sewn in a figure-eight stitch through two signatures. The paper cover was glued over the spine and a quarter inch onto the front and back pages. **lou:** variant spelling of "loo," a card game.

Tuesday 16 A very biting cold day. ¶Went over to Crane's shop in the morning, and got $25, which I did not expect to get, and am so much in, to recompense me for the losses of last night. Not able to deliver the rest of the pamphlets, because the binder—curse him—went back on me again. ¶At the Rink in the evening, to a grand masquerade. It is very singular that I never learned to skate or dance or do anything in the pleasure line.

Crane's: There is no advertiser by this name in the pamphlet. Perhaps this was an owner or employee of one of the advertisers, or a purchaser of some of the pamphlets.

Wednesday 17 Collected my bill against Col. Bowen, and was lucky enough to get a pass to Monmouth and Quincy, on the C.B. & Q.R.R. ¶At the Rink in the evening, seeing the Meaghers skate: Young, the younger, has succeeded in prejudicing them against me, through the machinations of Chas. Aug. ¶Took the midnight train for Monmouth, and went into a berth in sleeping car. My slumber was fitful, because of the different thoughts that filled my aching brain.

Col. Bowen: James Harvey Bowen, one of the three brothers who owned "Bowen Brothers Importers in Dry Goods." They had a full-page ad in both editions of the Stock Yards pamphlet. **C.B. & Q.R.R.:** Chicago Burlington & Quincy Railroad.

Thursday 18 Arrived at Monmouth at 9 o'clock, and went to THE REVIEW office. The general appearance of the town is far ahead of Kankakee. The office is a good one for a country town, and I am well pleased with it. Everything looks favorable to me, and Swain offers to sell me half at $1,200, one half down, and a note for the rest. Arranged to meet him in Chicago Tuesday, and started for Quincy. Arrived there, went to the Tremont and met Chas Gurley, my old Poki chum.

Chas Gurley: See 7/26/65. **Poki:** Pulaski, N.Y.

Friday 19 It is strange how my very existence was once wrapped up in this same little Gurley, for whose society I now care so little! It is an inexplicable mystery of my nature. ¶Charley got a carriage and we rode around town some. The day passed anything but pleasantly. Called at the newspaper offices but could get no sight for anything. And so between hopes and fears, the day passed, until train time, when I left the Mississippi country far behind. A violent storm came on, the car rocked and the attendant darkey's hair stood on end.

Saturday 20 Arrived at my room about 7 1/2 o'clock; one of the coldest mornings of my existence. ¶Sold my gas stove to Colbert of the TRIBUNE for $16, and immediately replaced it with a coal burner for $27, which I borrowed some coal and set burning. ¶Passed the day between doubts and fears. Am not yet able to make up my mind whether to go to Monmouth or not. O! for someone to tell me which is the best! ¶Finally decided that I would *not* go; but the future only knows.

Sunday 21 Managed to start a fire in my new stove this morning, and kept it burning all day, by dint of stealing coal. ¶Met A. T. Skinner; the whilom pedagouge of H[olmes].V[ille]. at the Briggs House, who is traveling for a house in the east. He dined with me, and then went to my room; and we talked over times that are passed. Met him at the Sherman House at 7 o'c. and took tea with him; after which spent a very pleasant evening in his room, with Whitman. ¶Retired to my v[irtuous] couch alone.

H.V.: W is surely referring to Pulaski, N.Y., where he went to school, as there was no school in Holmesville. **with Whitman:** This is most likely an acquaintance of W, perhaps the Whittman mentioned on 5/31/66, rather than a reference to reading some of the poetry of Walt Whitman (1819–92).

Monday 22 The morning to commence work for the Travellers Ins. Co. if I accept the position offered me. Found the secretary sick, and so did not go to work. ¶The day wore away, and I endured it. To-morrow Swain, of THE MONMOUTH REVIEW will be here, and I must decide about buying his office. O! for the good fates to advise. My life has been one continual struggle with adversity, with an occasional bright ray of prosperity, which has shown out only to be eclipsed by a fresh tide of disappointment. O! poor Jack Wing.

Tuesday 23 Met Swain; he has concluded *not* to sell. This is an entirely new phase. He has been at THE TIMES office, and they have been raking down on me. ¶Well, I thank Fortune that it is so. Visions of desolate Monmouth disperse—for, the Lord knows what. ¶Decided to go to Waukegan and look at the GAZETTE office. Embarked and arrived there. The place is fresh in my memory with the hanging of Bell last summer. ¶Cary has a splendid office—power presses, etc. Offered him $2,000 for half of it—$1,000 down and the remainder in 2 years.

Bell: see 6/30/65. **Cary:** James Y. Cary, the owner of the *Waukegan Gazette*.

Wednesday 24 Spent the entire day in looking over THE GAZETTE office. It is one of the best country establishments I ever saw; has facilities for fine job work, and a nice counting room and safe. Cary took me up at my offer and I paid him $25 to bind the bargain, agreeing to return next week, bag and baggage, and take possession—the co-partnership to date from Feb 1st. ¶Now the Lord only knows how I am to raise $1,000. But it *must* be forthcoming. ¶Inserted an advertisement of my room for sale in the *Tribune.*

job work: printing jobs for ephemera such as posters, tickets, and announcements of various kinds. **room for sale:** W's room ad appeared this day in the *Chicago Tribune*: "To Rent | A room and furniture . . . Room No 20, Tyler block, on LaSalle St. between Lake & South Water. . . . will accomodate two or more if necessary. . . ."

Thursday 25 At noon received several applications for my room, but the parties are not pleased with it. Some are too fastidious to live up so high, and it is not furnished well enough for them—while it costs too much for others. ¶I almost despair of selling it for anything—and yet I *must* get enough for it to make out $1,000, besides my $650 in the bank. ¶Night came, and I am no nearer selling than this morning. As a *denir* resort, again advertised it, and went to bed with many gloomy reflections.

Friday 26 No hope until noon and then recieved a note from parties on Lake Street. Took them up to see it, and by dint of bantering and agreeing to have my guitar, pictures, etc. they agreed to take it for $250. ¶Went to work boxing up my books, and packing my trunk. The dear old room of my prosperity and adversity is soon transformed. It is no longer mine, and I am no longer of Chicago. O! how strange does my fortune work! ¶Went to the opera and saw Forrest in Damon & Pythias—grand.

guitar: W was interested in performing as well as listening to music, and had taken singing lessons back in New York where he also taught himself to play the guitar and melodeon (a small reed organ). **Forrest:** Edwin Forrest (1806–72), "earliest American-born actor of the first rank

. . . . In 1866 he played to $2,500 a night in Chicago. . . ." (Johnson and Malone [eds], *Dictionary of American Biography*). Forrest played Damon. **Damon & Pythias:** a five-act tragedy by John Banim (1798–1842). A favorite of Forrest, he published several acting editions of this play between the 1840s and the 1870s.

Saturday 27 Made over my policy of insurance to Handy & Stickney, and they gave me a check for $250. Got my baggage to the depot, and everything is readiness for my hegira to Waukegan. Drew my money, and find that all I can raise is $900. Went to the pawnbroker Jacobs, and pawned my diamond pin, giving him a note for $105 at 30 days, and got $100—which makes my $1,000. Took a sad adieu of the only place where I have known prosperity, and started for Waukegan. Arrived there, and went to Cary's house to spend the evening.

Handy & Stickney: No company by this name is found in the city directories for 1865, 1866, or 1867. Perhaps W miswrote this for Handy & Hinckley, a commercial merchant firm in the Chamber of Commerce building. **hegira:** Muhammad's flight from Mecca to Medinah in 622 C.E., hence a journey or exodus. W may have discovered this unusual word in a headline for an article he wrote for the *Times* on 7/17/65. **Jacobs:** Edward Jacobs, proprietor of the Equitable Loan Office at 65 State Street. **$105 at 30 days:** a monthly interest rate of five percent.

Sunday 28 My first Sunday in the country town, where like the fool that I am, I am about to cast my destiny. A duller day I have never known. Went to Church with the Cary's in the forenoon; and suffered through the afternoon, going to bed at 8 o'clock. ¶I am here, for weal or woe. Who would have thought it, a month ago! But O follow fate. ¶Wrote a letter to Annie, telling her where I am, and of my new arrangement. ¶And Jack Wing, the gay and stylish youth, is now J. M. Wing, a country editor.

Monday 29 Assumed the Chair, and prepared copy for the outside of Cary & Wing paper. ¶Am actually starving at that villanous hole, the Waukegan House. O! what a change from my dear old room; and what a change from Chicago! But I have made my bed, driven by stern necessity, and must lie in it, although it be thousands of miles from home and kin, and no

~~propsect~~ prospect of ever seeing them again ever presenting itself. ¶It was a long day, this; but an example of what the days here are to be for me.

Tuesday 30 It is hard telling how the days pass. I confine myself to the office, because there is no where else to go. Am studying to learn the way things are situated in the office. It is very plain. Cary's imbecile brother, Ben, is a pensioner upon the establishment, and takes money without asking for it. It will be a hard thing to shake him off, but it must be done. Succeeded in getting old purity Thayer and Bradbury discharged from the establishment. ¶The blue-devils have got a splendid hold on me now.

Thayer and Bradbury: probably compositors and pressmen. See the next entry and 2/8/66. **blue-devils:** depression.

Wednesday 31 My fourth day, and not a word from anybody by letter. Why should they write—they are little aware of where Jack Wing is. ¶Got the outside ready for the press. The paper bears the names of CARY & WING proprietors. Have I done well, or not? ¶Worked the first side off, doing some of the feeding myself. It works well and I like the press very much. Whether the office makes any money or not I dare not conjecture; I *know* it has facilities far ahead of most country offices.

Worked the first side off: printed the outside of the paper. As W had worked as a typesetter and pressman in upstate New York in the early 1860s, he was quite capable of doing this.

FEBRUARY

Thursday 1 To-day the thoughts of my incarceration in this town almost drove me mad. Home and dear mother, pinning away for me, and I so far away, overflowed me. I could not work, and writing was out of the question. ¶Told Cary that I was sick of my bargain, and that I had a mind to leave. He urged me to stay, and I consented! I know the horrors of the place hunting, and and dare not give up even this thing for more of those terrible days of nothing to do and expense. Went to a country surprise party in evening.

February 1866

Friday 2 So it wags on, in this dismal hole, where I seem to have cast my lot. Got up a sensation upon Rawlings, M.D. which a villager does not want printed. But decided to run the risk. ¶If any former period of my life has been dismal, it is now doubly so. Not even a mouse stirs in this doubly benighted town. I fear that I have incarcerated myself for life in a prison that I shall never like. ¶The long day passed, the Lord only knows how; and I, poor I, passed along with it. Our partnership commenced yesterday.

Saturday 3 THE GAZETTE is out this morning in flying colors. Cary makes a "business announcement," of selling to me, and I respond in a "Salutatory." Its general appearance is good, and I am well pleased with it; if I could only settle down to the stern reality of this town. ¶Mailed papers to all my old friends in the east, and to the papers asking for an exchange. ¶And thus my stay here is rivetted beyond the hope of escape. I cannot bear even to think upon it. So draw the curtain for to-day.

exchange: an exchange of newspapers, for the purpose of copying news items.

Sunday 4 Spent the entire forenoon in unpacking my trunk. Found it to be in a sad muddle indeed: but, thank fortune, none of the pictures are broken. Pictures! what shall I do with them now? ¶At the office in the afternoon and wrote several letters. Thus the day dragged itself away. But my sundays were always a bore: why complain of this! ¶I have got the Itch—the d—dest kind. I scratch when at work, when at my meals, and *dig* when in bed. I *rake* my poor flesh all night, and in truth, am I dying of it !!!

Itch: W has developed a case of psychosomatic eczema.

Monday 5 At the office preparing copy. How the day passed I cannot imagine. Published Farnsworth's speech this week on the outside, and much other valuable matter. ¶There seems to be very little use for me to attempt to prolong this history of my daily doings, for now there is no "doings." One ceaseless round of monotony. I feel as if I would rather sacrifice the hard earned money I paid for this shop, than stay in this damnable town another day!

Farnsworth's speech: John F. Farnsworth (1820–97), Canadian-born politician and soldier; Republican member from Illinois of the U.S. House of Representatives from 1857 to 1861. He served in the war as a colonel in the 8th regiment, Illinois Volunteer Cavalry, from 1862 to 1863, when he returned to the House, where he served until 1873.

Tuesday 6 I'm discouraged. This seems to be the end of Jack Wing. In a country town, in a worse country office, life is worse than a blank. There is a sting in death, and there is a scorpion's sting in staying here. ¶Asked Cary to pay me back a portion of my money, and let me go. But he has got too soft a thing on me and wont do it, not he. ¶I retire filled with the most gloomy and discouraged thoughts. But it's not the first time I've had such thoughts—O! no!

too soft a thing on me: has the advantage of him. See 2/9/66.

Wednesday 7 Time was when I prided myself upon my *hauteur*—my get up. But O Ye Gods! what now do I most desire—what most do I take to heart. When I arise in the morning I have scarce ambition to put on my trousers. The day ahead of me is all a meaningless blank. ¶The four dingy walls of this country office encircle me. Here is a doleful picture of Abraham Lincoln, draped in crape, as black as the drapery of my own sorrowful heart. A pile of country exchanges confronts me on the table. "All this, and nothing more."

Thursday 8 I am growing daily and daily nearer mortification. I feel the blood cooling around my heart. There is not enough excitement to make it beat. It's so still here that if it was spring time one might hear the shooting forth of the grass and flowers. ¶I think!—No I muse in utter abstractions. Now I recollect that there is still life in my poor carcas, and I drag myself into the other room, and observe the process of setting type, performed by two devils and a sub. It's all strange to me, because I am grown an enigma to myself.

two devils: apprentices.

February 1866

Friday 9 Press-day, yet very like yesterday, very like what tomorrow will be. ¶Superintended making up the sheet—sat like a young Ben Franklin upon a tripod, and dictated where to put the matter. ¶Told Cary that I could not stay here—that I was slowly dying of the town—but he has got too soft a thing on me. I'm in his clutches, and he is well aware of the fact. It surely was some ill fate which drove me here. I am almost determined to give him my first $1,000 and be again a free man!

Saturday 10 Went to Chicago. It is no longer a place where I delight to be. It's a foreign land now—I have notheing there. Played out is the term. But I took $1,000 out of it, only to sink it in the stagnant pool around about the Gazette office. Returned at night, more downcast than ever. ¶Recd a letter, that had been advertised, from Harv Hoffman, a Clinton YB, directed to me as Assistant City Ed. *The Chicago Times*! Ye Gods, how the old time comes oe'r us! ¶Also received a letter from Anna, the first since I have been here.

advertised: addressed.

Sunday 11 Sunday! ¶An infliction—a damnable torment to me. In Chicago it was bad enough—here it is a hell! I mean what I say, ye follower of Christ, should this fall beneath your vision. While I am cursed as I am now, Sunday adds torment to my caged soul. ¶O! for Wings!! [Line space] ¶Spent the entire day like a mule—without one moment [of] enjoyment. It's my tormented soul that's eating me up. It demands work, recompense, excitement, anything!!

Monday 12 A letter from dear Brick Pomeroy, dated at Walnut Hill, is a bright oasis in this dreary desert of life. Mine is a warm heart for those I love—but a bitter one to those I hate. Deck is the concentration of all my better feelings. I love him as wildly, passionately as I might that gentle girl whose devotions I once despised. And partly too, because he knew her, and knows of our love. Wrote him—O! such a letter. ¶But that is all. The rest of the day is a blank, unruled by a single occurrence, a single event.

Brick: This is the YB Dick (or Deck) Pomeroy, but W is probably making a jocular reference to the famous nineteenth-century newsman, Marcus Mills "Brick" Pomeroy. Pomeroy had founded the La Crosse, Wis., *Democrat* in 1860 and made it a leading midwestern newspaper. **Walnut Hill:** school in upstate New York that had many YB fraternity members. **gentle girl:** Fan Churchill.

Thursday 15 When I hastily cast my lot in this d—d town, I was a consummate fool, and that is something I never admitted myself to be before. ¶Have I described it in this authentic record. Here goes then for posterity: ¶Waukegan is a four corner, on Lake Michigan. Its inhabitants are Indians, its houses built of brush and straw. At least so it appears to me. Its original plan was that of a penitentiary, but Joliet got the preference, in view of the fact that the convicts could not live out their terms of imprisonment here.

four corner: a crossroad.

Friday 16 Press day, and THE WAUKEGAN GAZETTE is prepared to go forth to its 800 Lake County farmers. They will read it to-morrow as so much scripture, and thus it will end. If the print is too small for the optics of some blind Dame Elenor Spearing, then we shall surely lose a subscriber. Perhaps a farmer may find a word in it he does not like, then he will stop *his* paper too. ¶This is the history of country journalism. A bigoted farmer is the most detestable being on earth. He is small minded, and small pocketed.

Dame Elenor Spearing: A character in Thomas Hood's poetry. See 9/28/65, for W's purchase of a quarto edition of Hood's poems.

Saturday 17 Went to Chicago on the 10 o'clock train, and spent most of the day in canvassing. Got several jobs, and a little advertising. ¶Talked with Cary about letting me off. He is so d—d hard up that his creditors have perfectly absorbed the $1,000 I paid him, and I am the loser. He is willing for me to go i but wants me to give him what I have paid on the office. I am then left in a very pretty fix. ¶Fate has again turned against me, and I am now in danger of losing my first $1,000.

Sunday 18 The itch. It's got a close hold on my poor cuticle, and is eating me up by slow degrees. "Purigho Lotio" is of little avail. My hands look like elephant's ears—ditto my arms and legs. Poor Penis—virtuous appendage of a virtuous youth—has not escaped the general rupturing. Pustules filled with hot water between my toes, and at the roots of every hair. ¶The gout, the plague, small pox—anything would be acceptable in proper season; but the prarie itch endureth forever. O! woe is me!!

"Purigho Lotio": Prurigo Lotio was advertised as "The Great Itch and Humor Killer of the 19th Century." It cost fifty cents a bottle.

Monday 19 Went to Chicago again, in order to pass away the day. But it is all a blank to me there now. Behold, I have no abiding place in the new Jerusalem. ¶Another week. How is it to be passed. Here by this accursed table—pouring over a poor pipe and miserable tobacco. ¶Now and then a farmer comes in, and leaves a few shillings. The aggregate for the day may reach $1.50—not more. When Saturday night comes, that will not be enough money to pay the devil for his week's work. This is the "business" of this office.

devil: apprentice.

Tuesday 20 I have been basely deceived. Instead of this office paying, as I was told, it runs behind $25 every week. And there is nothing to bring it up. Life here is worse than death. The stillness of the town stifles the senses. I am the victim of utter despondency, and of the most terrible *ennui:* I feel as if I was at the end of my course: anchored at last to a forlorn hope. And as yet I see no means of Cutting lose; none but to sacrifice my first $1,000 and dig for other and more favorable climes.

dig: depart.

Wednesday 21 The Atlantic for March is my solace to-day. ¶In the afternoon saw from the window a boy with a city cut and city walk. Made for him and found a pleasant fellow, clerk in a house in Chicago. Froze to him, like a drowning man to a straw. He spent the evening in the office. Anybody to speak to now. I could converse with a stevedor, if he had ever seen town. ¶Changed my lodgings for to-night back to the rat closet of the

Waukegan House. Company at Cary's and my bed in demand.

The Atlantic: In addition to prose, poems, and essays by authors that would scarcely be recognized today (B. W. Ball, William Parker, Mrs. L. M. Child, Charles Reade, among others), this issue also contained "Passages from [Nathaniel] Hawthorne's Note-Books," and Harriet Beecher Stowe's column, "The Chimney-Corner for 1866." **city cut:** urban tailoring.

Thursday 22 This is the IX volume of the graphic and authentic history of my poor and simple, yet ambitious life, and I have never had its pages so far behind before. I have now absolutely forgotten what occurred at this date, but am very safe in saying that it was all quiet. A farmer might have come into the office during the day—all this and nothing more. ¶I watch the mails now with desperation. Nothing comes, even for The Gazette. Friends soon forget one, when one forgets himself so far as to immure himself as I have done.

and nothing more: perhaps an allusion to "The Raven" by Edgar Allen Poe (1809–49). First published in 1845, this poem quickly became a popular success.

Friday 23 A little excitement, even in Waukegan, to-day. Andy Johnson has turned tail on his party, and gone over to the Copperheads. He made a speech in front of the White House last night, saying that the Republicans thirsted for his (Andy's) blood, and all that sort of twaddle. The whole country is convulsed. He was either drunk or insane—Perhaps both. ¶Press day again. Cary and I have a set-to about an article on Johnson. It's the same old story—a country paper must not express an opinion. ¶The papers off—and I off.

Andy Johnson: Andrew Johnson (1808–75), U.S. president from 1865 to 1868. Johnson's speech, made the previous day, was against supporting a civil-rights act to give the vote to former slaves.

Saturday 24 To add to my other ills, my despondency and my *itch*, another bile has made its appearance, this time on my hip, just far enough around to be out of the sight of my eyes, and consequently beyond my control. It's my direful fate. A modern Job—but a d—d impatient one. ¶Slept at the house on the sofa after dinner, and nursed my bile. Finally crept down to the office, and crept back again to go to bed. This is history here; this is daily life. Get up—sit at the office, see a farmer or two, go home, go to bed. My God! a Paradise!

bile: boil.

Sunday 25 I'm a hell of a fellow here. I was a correspondent of the N.Y. *Herald* during the war, of course I was. I have fought, bled and died for—Jack Wing. I have also seen New York [City] and "the Hub," as well as having lived at the "Fourth Operatic Centre." I am the author of "Kilgubbin & Kansas." ¶So do I exalt myself among the heathen. So do I claim, when there is none to question. I'm a hypocrite, that's what ails me. ¶Sunday. Ate, slept and worked my feet. Itch on the increase—scratched.

"the Hub": Boston. **"Fourth Operatic Centre":** Chicago? **"Kilgubbin & Kansas":** These were the names of the shanty towns in W's controversial article on the Chicago Irish. See 8/6/65 and Appendix C.

Monday 26 I lived an age to-day. Dogged old Cary to let me off, to refund to me a portion of my dues, and let me leave this accursed hole. But he is not inclined to hear me. He prefers to keep his soft thing. If I get off at all, it will be by the very skin of my teeth. ¶But where, O! where! if I get free here, with a few hundred dollars saved out of my $1,000—my first loved, treasured lucre? The question embarrasses me more than any other. But there are yet climes untried, seas unsailed, and desert sands untracked. There is also as good fish in the sea as ever were caught.

Tuesday 27 Intended to go to Chicago to-day, but am determined not to leave for a moment before Cary gives me some satisfaction about buying me off. ¶Stayed in the dreary office all day, and just at night got Cary to the point. He will not raise me any money, and says I have no business to go. Finally got him to say that he would "raise $300 if possible," and that "when he could." ¶Loafed around this d—d hole all day, with the most despairing feelings—almost suicidal.

Wednesday 28 Went to Chicago on the 10 o'clock train. Was fortunate enough to get passes to and from Detroit, and also to collect $300 of my dues. Every moment I spent there made me long for city life again. And I will have it! ¶Returned. Cary says he has not raised the money. What am I to do. Fate is in possession of the dark book of my future, and will use it to my weal or woe. But thank God; my dear old home—be it ever so humble—lies far away in the East, and there I can at lest find rest of body, if not of mind.

collect $300: money from advertisers and sales of the second edition of the Stock Yards pamphlet.

MARCH

Thursday 1 A painful day of doubts and fears. ¶The monotony of the forenoon was varied by a letter from Bronky, Hoffman and old Al Ingalls, my associate of the old "Roman Citizen." He wants a "sit" in the office. How mysterious do things come around! ¶Dreamed through the afternoon, in hopes that Cary would do something. But he is cold and don't care a d—d. ¶One thing is evident. The first $1,000 of my life has gone. But I am no worse off than I was when I returned from the East—nor so bad.

"sit": situation.

Friday 2 Went to Chicago and settled up my business there, and got my pants, paying $10 on them, and owing $6. ¶Cary has finally come to the conclusion that I really intend to leave here, and so gets me a check for $300. In the evening we settled up the thing. I took three notes for $200 each, due respectively in three, six and eight months. Thus I lose just $100 on this adventure. But I thank heaven to be let off this easily. Whether the notes are good or not remains to be seen.

Saturday 3 My heart beats lighter this morning than for many, many days before, and I feel like a risen spirit. ¶Got my check cashed and went to Chicago. Paid Jacobs the $100 I owed him, and got my diamond pin. Seeing a gem of a diamond ring, I got it of the old man, and gave a promissory note for $60 for it. I cut an enormous swell with it. My present condition shall never be known in the east. ¶And now for a time—now for a tramp.

Sunday 4 Returned to this benighted town to pack my trunk, and pass away the Sabbath. Spent the entire forenoon in getting myself in shape to start. My plan is to go to Detroit, and try to get a sit[uation] on the new *Post;* to visit Billy Bissell & Bob Tyrrel, having an extensive time generally. Then go on to Rochester, Walnut Hill, and Albany, making a short visit home in the mean time. Then as my funds grow short, return west and lay for a situation, going if not successful elsewhere, to St. Louis and New Orleans. And may Fate prosper me!

Monday 5 Farewell! ¶There are times when this word is fraught with soulless *nonchalance,* and when it carries misery and pains to the lacerated heart. On this occasion it is the former. I shake Cary—my whilom partner—by the hand, and go out from THE WAUKEGAN GAZETTE establishment. Cary & Wing has now returned to the James Y. Cary from whence it sprung. And I am a Wanderer—free as a beggar, with my portmanteau on my arm. ¶Arrived at Chicago, dined at Briggs House, called at *Tribune* office, and took the M.C.RR cars for Detroit.

M.C.RR: Michigan Central Railroad.

[W returns east to upstate New York for the rest of March and, on his return west, gets a position on the *Detroit Post* for a few days. The founder and editor-in-chief of the *Post* was General Carl Schurz (1829–1906). Born in Germany, Schurz, who served in the Civil War, became a newspaperman in 1865.]

APRIL

Tuesday 3 Not feeling able to take a sleeping car last night, I suffered terribly, and when the train arrived at Chicago this morning, I was nearly dead. My feet had swollen so that I could not get my shoes on, without the greatest difficulty. ¶Went at once to the Lloyd House—once my happy home—and went to bed. Got up to dinner and went to Tony's for a shave. Calling at THE TRIBUNE I soon learned that there was no hope for me getting work on the press here. ¶Went to the Theatre, Col Woods, where I still pass as a dead head, and I spent a rather pleasant evening.

Theatre: Col. Wood's was presenting "A new London comedy," *Black Sheep* by Joseph S. Coyne (1803–68) and an old Irish farce, *Horse Railroad* by Isaac Pocock (1782–1835).

Wednesday 4 Met Binmore, and he told me he could put me on the track of a position in New Orleans. Spent the entire day in looking it up, and in getting credentials, with a view of going there. It is my only hope. ¶Jacobs took back the diamond ring, and gave me my note. And so I have been enabled, by a little strategy, to get the wear of it for an entire month, to astonish the natives in the east; and I did it effectually. They thought me little short of a nabob.

Binmore: See 9/10/65. **diamond ring:** See 3/3/66 for this loan.

Thursday 5 To-day I have fully made up my mind to go to New Orleans, and strike for weal or woe. I have a letter from Jacobs, an old resident of New Orleans, to Holbrook, the proprietor of THE PICAYUNE, which may possibly be of some little avail to me. Have also got a letter from Colbert, of the TRIBUNE, as to my general qualifications. And I have also got left ~~a~~ $150.000, which is barely sufficient. But I shall venture it; and I will at least see the grand scenery down the Father of Waters, even if I return to Chicago dead broke.

Jacobs: Probably the pawnbroker mentioned in the previous entry. **Colbert:** the commercial editor of the *Tribune*. See 12/24/65. **$150.000:** W has written one too many zeroes after the decimal.

Friday 6 Today witnesses the launching forth of the proprietor of this veracious journal for the "Sunny South." Of what avail it shall be, the future alone can tell. But I believe my lucky star will yet rule. ¶Made all things ready for my journey. Wrote a letter to Philip, at Memphis, telling him I would soon be there. Also mailed a letter home. ¶Left the Lloyd House at 7 o'clock, and was soon en route to St. Louis. Met Andrews, of the *Peoria Transcript,* who gave me encouragement as to a position there.

Philip: unidentified, but likely a YB. **Andrews:** E. Andrews would become a partner in Sheffield, Wing & Co. advertising agency in St. Louis.

[The next day, on his twenty-second birthday, Wing buys a steamship ticket and on the 11th starts down the Mississippi to New Orleans. He fails to get a newspaper position there, and returns to St. Louis on the 27th, where he also fails to find a reporting job. He then begins an advertising agency with N. M. Sheffield, E. Andrews, and others. The partnership is dissolved on October 26, but W makes several trips to Chicago while living in St. Louis. The following entries record those visits.]

MAY

Thursday 31 Up and started for Chicago—the only place where I ever made any money. Collected $15 of Whittman on an old Gazette office account, and got some things of Walshe on same act. Every thing worked well—saw Jim Chisholm of old. Dined at Kinsley's on a steak, and luxuriated upon strawberries. Found several letters for me at the Lloyd, among them a dispatch from Davenport, of the Detroit Post, telling me to "come on the next train at $10 per week["]—how strange things work out. Left for St. Louis at 8 o'clock, and this time got a sleeping car. Traded pipes at Tremont House.

Whittman: Probably Charles E. Whitman, a Chicago dealer in agricultural implements. **Jim Chisholm:** See 7/19/65 and 11/23/65.

[W spends all of June and July in St. Louis setting up his advertising agency and seeking clients for it.]

AUGUST

Thursday 9 Arrived at the old Briggs House, and did not have a red cent after paying my buss fare. Canvassed all the morning for our prospected St Louis Fair Reporter, but had no success whatever. ¶Succeeded in getting my pay $40, of the Post, a god-send to me, in my present plight. ¶The day was a pretty long one, and starting for Waukegan I met Cary, and so did not go. ¶At 9 o'clock I was *en route* for St Louis, returning played out, and dissatisfied for having gone.

St Louis Fair Reporter: an advertising paper for the fourteenth annual Illinois State Fair. **my pay:** W had been writing up St. Louis market reports for the *Chicago Post.* **Cary:** W must have been headed to Waukegan to collect money from his erstwhile partner, Cary.

[W returns to St. Louis.]

Monday 13 Arrived at Briggs House and "Sam"—the name of my new chum—got left on the M.S.R.R. and so stayed over with me. I started out canvassing, and during the day took $75 of advertising for the fair Reporter, which I considered pretty well. ¶In evening Sam and I went to Col Wood's and after theatre met Al Ingalls, of the "Old Roman Citizen," much to my surprise. Took them both to Kinsley's and enjoyed it well. Then Sam and I went to bed, at Briggs, and had a splendid time.

M.S.R.R.: Michigan Southern Railroad. **Col Wood's:** *Moses in Egypt; or, Israel in Bondage,* a biblical spectacle specially written for Wood's theater by George L. Aiken (1830–76), was playing. **Al Ingalls:** W had received a letter from Al Ingalls asking about a "sit" in Chicago on 3/1/66. **"Old Roman Citizen":** W had worked on this paper in upstate New York in 1863.

Tuesday 14 I was aroused early by Sammy's saying "Good by Jack, I will write, old boy," and he was off. Dear fellow, when and where shall I see him again? ¶After breakfast went vigorously at work canvassing and had the most brilliant success. Taylor gave me a $75 ad. and during the day I took over $100, or worth, and laid the foundation for some more. ¶Went around to the theater in evening, but feeling tired went to bed early.

theater: W may have seen *Moses in Egypt* again, since that was still playing at Wood's, or maybe *The Falls of Clyde,* a two-act musical melodrama with a libretto by George Soane (1790–1860) and music by —? Cooke, and two monologues by Professor Silvestre—perhaps the American dramatist Paul Armand Silvestre (1837–1901)—at the McVicker's.

Wednesday 15 Canvassing again this morning, and met with good success. Took $65 worth of adv in the forenoon. Everybody seems desirous of putting off giving their orders until nearer fair time, and so I think I will go back to St Louis for a short time. Went to the *Post,* and got Haskell to write me a line to Hale of the C & St L R. R. He did it so badly that I had no little difficulty in getting a pass. But finally got one, and started for home on the 9 o'-clock train. Went to bed at once.

Haskell: William Haskell, bookkeeper at the *Chicago Post*. **Hale:** John Hale, general baggage agent. **C & St L R. R.:** Chicago & St. Louis Railroad. **pass:** W occasionally obtained free railroad passes by pretending to be a reporter when he was not.

[W stays in St. Louis until September 13.]

SEPTEMBER

Thursday 13 At Chicago! There is encouragement in the word, for here have I made what little reputation or character I have. The morning is rainy, and I go to the Matteson House, and there take up my quarters. After breakfast sallied forth and canvassed with all my might all day, and succeeded pretty well. But there is yet scarcely a beginning to the amt of advertising the sheet will contain. Went to the Museum in the evening.

Matteson House: This hotel was two doors east of Col. Wood's Museum on the northwest corner of Randolph and Dearborn. **Museum:** Col. Wood's Theatre and Museum. W may have dropped in to see the second half of the bill, *The Lottery Ticket* by John B. Buckstone, since he only mentions the top of the bill on 9/15/66.

Friday 14 Up early, and at work canvassing. Did not succeed quite as well as yesterday, but still secured enough advertising to place the success of "*The Daily Fair Reporter*" beyond the shadow of doubt. ¶Wrote to Andrews that he must come and help me. ¶Met several old newspaper boys, and was treated pretty well by them. ¶The day was drizzly, and I worked as if my life depended upon it. But prospects brighten up, and a gleam of sunshine appears.

Saturday 15 To-day met a fellow from Syracuse N.Y. one Hoyt, whom I once met there with Ed Spaulding. The sequel will tell what renewing his acquaintance amounted to. ¶Another long day of canvassing, with Fair success. Secured considerable more advertising, and put on my "bib and tucker" for the theatre in the evening, with considerable encouragement. ¶The "Invisible Prince" on the Boards at the Colonels, and a d—d big hit it is too.

Spaulding: a YB friend of W's. **"bib and tucker":** formal clothes. **"Invisible Prince":** First performed in London in 1846, this one-act "extravaganza" was by James Robinson Planché (1796–1880). If Planché is known at all today, it is as the librettist for Carl Maria von Weber's opera *Oberon*.

Sunday 16 A Sunday away from one's headquarters, is more dull than anything else. Loafed around the Matteson House nearly all day. ¶The afternoon was cloudy and gloomy, with indications of rain. Having no overcoat, I found it rather chilly, and consoled my self with the hope that I soon will have one, if my fair paper is a success. ¶In the evening met Guy MaKee, Chisholm and several other Bohemians & managed to while away the time.

Guy Makee: W's phonetic spelling of Guy Magee, a reporter for the *Tribune*. In 1910 W dedicated one of his extra-illustrated books to him (*Habits and Men* by John Doran) and included in it an autographed photograph of Magee as an old man. **Bohemians:** fellow members of the reporters' club. See 9/10/65.

Monday 17 At work canvassing with a will, and my endavors were rewarded by placing several new names in my contract Books. ¶Receive a letter from Andrews, who says that he will be here on Wednesday morning. ¶Rainy in the afternoon. Called on Jerry Thompson who directs me to the Republican office to get my Fair paper out, as Higgie his old foreman has just taken it.

Jerry Thompson: See 12/4/65. **has just taken it:** has become the printing manager of the *Republican*.

Tuesday 18 Go to *Republican* office—my old place of labor and the scene of my Dr Mack feud—and get figures upon the job from Higgie which are much lower than I expected. ¶Kept on Canvassing with some littel success. Still, the paper is not one quarter full. ¶Am having one of the largest times here on record. Fell in with a bully boy from Detroit, went to Museum with him, and then he went and stayed with me at the Matteson House. A gay duck.

Dr Mack feud: see 1/5/66. **Museum:** *Two Can Play That Game*, a translation and adaptation of the French comedy *Livre III, Chap. 1* by Eugène

A. Pierron (1819–65) and Adolphe Lafferrière, opened this evening and was playing with *The Invisible Prince.*

Wednesday 19 Andrews arrives this morning before I am up, much to my delight. The old cuss is right on it, and after breakfast starts off on a canvassing tour. ¶Run against Ingalls of Rome remembrances, & he agrees to help me through with the Fair paper. This relieves my mind of considerable excitement. ¶Sabey of Syracuse in town again, stopping at Sherman House. Dined with him, went around town in evening, and finally after wine at Kinsleys go to bed with him at Sherman House.

Ingalls: Al Ingalls, a friend of W from New York. See 8/13/66 for a previous encounter with Ingalls in Chicago.

Thursday 20 Sabey up and off on train at 6 1/2, leaving me in bed. Soon the porter and Clerk come up and raise a row, wanting to know how the hell I got there, etc. ¶Canvassing again, reading proof on paper, etc. Andrews has pretty fair success canvassing. We get a livery team and go around through the mud, to my infinite disgust. I get a column out of the Chicago Scale Co. for which I am to take a hay scale (!) Andrews left in the evening for St Louis.

Friday 21 So I am left alone to fill up the paper and get it out. It is a big job, but *must* succeed. Got a $25.00 ad from the Prairie Farmer. Canvassed all day, with fair success. ¶Sabey returns in the afternoon, bringing several Chummies, one of whom had a female with him at the Sherman House. We had a big time there in the evening—one of the largest on Record. ¶To-morrow night I shall have the first No of "The Daily Reporter."

Saturday 22 Devoted the entire day to hard canvassing and arranging forms and the make up of the Reporter. Secured a few advertisements, and at six o'clock had the satisfaction of getting a proof of the outside, which looks bully in the extreme. ¶My hard canvassing is now at an end, but the labor of fair week is yet before me, with all its accompanying horrors. ¶Sabey & Co started again for Milwaukee, to return next week. ¶At theatre in the evening. Col's.

forms and the make up: printing terms for set type and page layout. **Col's:** Perhaps W saw *The Invisible Prince* once more, since it was still playing with *Two Can Play That Game*. See 9/18/66.

Sunday 23 A long Sunday of anxious waiting between doubts and fears as to the success of the Reporter. ¶Ingalls came down to Matteson House in the morning, and we arranged about the circulation. He is to have entire charge of it: hire boys, etc. This relieves my mind of much. ¶Around with the Bohemians in the evening, visiting some of my old haunts about town. I can scarcely imagine why I left here: but still what else could I do!

Monday 24 Up early and at the press room of the *Republican* office, anxious beyond words to see the first impression of The *Daily Fair Reporter.* When it appeared I was very well pleased with it. ¶Got the edition off after much delay, and Ingalls, with a squad of boys started for the Fair Grounds. They had hardly left in the street cars, when the rain commenced to pour down in torrents, so that I did not follow them out, as I expected too. And the rain continued all day.

***Daily Fair Reporter*:** See 8/9/66.

Tuesday 25 Early at the office again, and got Ingalls off to the fair grounds with the papers. It still kept raining, but I followed him out. Arriving there all was a sea of slush and mud. The *Reporter* lay around in the rain without readers, or any one to pocket them. ¶Discouraged and heart sick I went down to the office, and dished up a meager report for to-morrow.

Wednesday 26 A cheerful, bright morning, with fresh pure air. Saw the III No of *The Daily Fair Reporter* start for the fair grounds, with much better feeling. ¶Went out to the Fair grounds myself and was gratified to see the paper growing popular among the visitors and also the offices. ¶In the afternoon the Western Rural man came in, and paid me five dollars for a local puff. There begin to be many calls to see me at the counting room, and I begin to feel pretty well again.

the Western Rural man: untraced.

Thursday 27 The 4th Number of The Reporter. ¶Out on the fair grounds early, and vigorously at work canvassing for local puffs—Collected in about $20 for them, and went down to the office to have them set up. ¶Had I but one of my partners—whom I am thus helping to support—here to help me, there might be twice as much made out of such things. ¶Went to the Colonels in the evening, feeling pretty well, as a little success always makes me feel.

Colonels: *The Invisible Prince* was still playing, along with *The Boots at the Swan* by Charles Selby (1802?–63).

Friday 28 Another beautiful day and the fair a grand success. Early out there, and by noon had my efforts crowned by collecting about $90.00 for local puffs. THE REPORTER is everywhere upon the grounds. I ought to have had an office there; for it would have materially enhanced my interests. The other fair paper, *The Mirror* does not amount to a row of beans. ¶In the evening, I found a Detroit boy, who agreed to go home with me, but Bolshaws Whiskey-stinger interfered, for which I should like to shoot the pup.

No copies of either *The Mirror* or *The Daily Fair Reporter* have survived. **found a Detroit boy:** W must have met him at the Matteson House, where Bolshaw ran the saloon. See 12/25/65. **Bolshaws Whiskey-stinger interfered:** The Detroit boy probably got drunk and was in no condition to go home with W.

Saturday 29 The Last Day of the Fair!! I have long looked for it. Out there in the morning, but saw none of the men who owed me. Drank wine with Supt Goltra, and got his approbation for publishing the Reporter next year. ¶In the afternoon commenced collecting, with good luck. Got in about a hundred dollars, and some of the trumpery which I took for advertising. ¶In the evening Sabey & Co returned. At Kinsleys saw the Churchill's of Rome, to my great surprise, who were there drinking wine.

Supt Goltra: M. C. Goltra, superintendent of the Illinois State Fair grounds. **the Churchill's:** the family of W's first girlfriend, Fan.

Sunday 30 Over to the Tremont house in the forenoon, and dined with Sabey. In afternoon we got a barouche and had a very gay ride out to Douglas grove, up and down the Avenues, etc. In the evening we paid a visit to the Mansion of Madame H— on State st, where many things occured which ill befit the pages of this authentic diary. We returned to the Tremont "in an early twilight of Hackney coach," and I turned in with the boys, determined to make an all night job of it. Sic transit.

Madame H—: no doubt a brothel. **"in an early twilight . . .":** I have not found the source of this quote.

OCTOBER

Monday 1 Collecting all day with fair success, but have not got more than half through. ¶Got a guitar at Bauers by paying $10.00 more than my bill for advertising, and also got a case of Higgins. ¶Last night when went to bed took a boy to sleep with me. He got up and went off early leaving the door unlocked. When I got up found my pocket book stolen, and my watch and chain saved by my awakening just as the thief was making off. Lost about $10.00, return pass to St L. etc.

Bauers: See 12/13/65.

Tuesday 2 Early to my work collecting. Managed to settle with the Chicago Scales Co., by taking one quarter of bill. ¶Got my new overcoat at Walshes, a splendid thing—the nicest one I ever owned in my life. Must get ready to go to St Louis to-morrow night sure. ¶All in all, if this thing belonged to me, I should make a nice little sum out of it. But as it is, I shall probably come off slim in money, although I may save something in the way of goods for myself. ¶Theatre in eve.

Walshes: Robert J. Walshe, a tailor who took an advertisement in W's Chicago Tunnel pamphlet. His shop was at 59 Clark Street, opposite the Sherman House. **Theatre:** W's choices were *Rob Roy: or, Auld Lang Syne,* an operatic drama adapted from Walter Scott with a libretto by Isaac Pocock (1782–1835) and music by J. Davy at Col. Wood's; *Fast People,* a translation by "a gentleman of Chicago" of *La Famille Beniton* by the contemporary French playwright Victorien Sardou (1831–1908) at the McVicker's; or the Kelly and Leon's Mistrels at the Academy of Music.

Wednesday 3 Collecting again, and getting things ready to start for St Louis. Got in all my bills but three, which are not now collectable. ¶Bought me a beautiful traveling rug, and with it and my new overcoat and Satchel, took the 9 o'clock train. It was crowded so that I did not get a sleeping car until about midnight, when I gladly secured a single birth, and turned in. My money $500.00, the proceeds of fair paper in my jacket.

[W returns to St. Louis, where he dissolves his partnership with Sheffield on October 26th.]

Monday 29 Once more in the Garden City, with my fortune to make. Quartered myself at the Matteson House and sallied out to collect the remaining fair paper bills. Failed in all save Dr Reynold's. Learned enough to convince me that to get on the *Times* is an impossibility. ¶Went up to Waukegan in afternoon, and got Cary to give me a receipt for the pamphlet printing and endorse it upon last note. Sheffield agreed to send me a draft if I would do so, but I have little faith in his honesty.

Dr Reynold's: B. Phillip Reynolds, a physician and surgeon whose offices were on the southwest corner of Madison and Dearborn streets.

Tuesday 30 Came down from the place where my first $1,000 was buried to the city where I made it. ¶Called upon Philips of the M.S.R.R. and got passes to Cleveland & return. Secured my sleeping birth, and got everything in readiness for another trip east, looking for something to turn up. ¶Sent Cary's receipt to Sheffield, writing him to send me a draft. ¶And am off [Rule] ¶From here date another important era in my vascillating life!

Philips: Elijah B. Philips, president of the Michigan Southern Railroad.

[W returns to the east coast for over three weeks, visiting Boston and New York City on his way back to Chicago.]

NOVEMBER

Friday 23 Jumped off the train at Clark street, and am at my old resort, when poverty overtakes me—the Lloyd House. Get breakfast, and go down town. It is cold and Cheerless, and my heart almost sinks within me. ¶Was lucky enough to get my revolver at the sleeping car office, which I lost coming down from St Louis. ¶Went to Republican office and find that Jerry Thompson is getting out a Holiday paper. Decide to go to Waukegan in the morning, and see if Cary will not print mine.

Clark street: W is a block off; the M.S.R.R. depot was actually at Van Buren and LaSalle streets.

Saturday 24 Awoke just time enough to get on my clothes and get to the depot for the train, without breakfast. Cary agrees to print the paper for me for $75, I finding the paper. I get a sample sheet and some blank contracts printed, and also a $10 card from D. L & Co. ¶Feeling quite elated at my success thus far, came back, and stopping into Martin's bookstore, got an ad from him for $15.00. Ascertain that L & K are also printing such a paper. Bed in cold at Lloyd House.

$10 card: advertisement. See 11/30/66. **D. L & Co.:** Leslie & Company Printers, near Crosby's Opera House. **Martin's bookstore:** Thomas W. Martin ran a bookstore at 91 Washington Street. **L & K:** Landon & Kroff Printers, on the southwest corner of Clark and Washington streets.

Sunday 25 No stove in my poor room, and a long, cold, dismal day, of doubts, hopes and fears. Did almost everything to pass it away, but it hung heavily. ¶Wrote a letter to Charlie Rogers, and one to Anna. ¶In evening went down to Nolan's room, and passed an hour very pleasantly. But it brings back the memory of my old room, and my past bad luck. ¶And to-morrow commences the race for Advertisements. I am sanguine that I will succeed well.

Charlie Rogers: Son of C. O. Rogers, publisher of the *Boston Journal*. W had met father and son on his return trip up the Mississippi from New Orleans in late April. **Nolan's room . . . my old room:** Perhaps E. Nolan, a printer who was boarding at the St. Cloud Hotel earlier in the year but who now seems to be living in Tyler's block. See 12/16/66.

Monday 26 Rain! Rain! ¶Sallie forth and go eagerly to work canvassing for the holiday paper. Find to my surprise that there is several already in the field, and that there is no chance for another. But keep at it all day. Succeed in getting an ad out of Grover & Baker, if I will take a sewing machine. This, and nothing more all day long. At night felt lonely & dejected. Did not know what to do. There is no chance for my Christmas sheet. Went down and talked with friend Walshe, the tailor.

Grover & Baker: a sewing machine manufacturer at 115 Lake Street.
Walshe: Robert J. Walshe. See 10/2/66.

Tuesday 27 My talk with Walshe last eve cleared up my drooping spirits, and I decided to give "The Western Dial["] a trial, getting it up after the style of one I saw in Boston. So I started for Waukegan this morning, and spent the entire day there, loafing around, as Kribbs could not go to work on the job. But he promised it to me on Saturday. Finally endure[d] out the time until the train arrives, and return to my Lloyd House lodgings in the mud and rain, more dejected than ever.

Wednesday 28 Resolved to do a little more in hopes to get through the Christmas sheet, but without success. ¶Resolved to make a trial on the Lake Tunnel history, and got figures on it. Went over to the tunnel and saw Col Gowan. He says that Hasmer of Tribune is getting out one. Thus am I constantly thwarted. But determined to put this through, if possible. And now am decided to lend all my energies to it, as my only hope. ¶Collected my bill against the Eagle Gas Stove Co $10.

Hasmer: untraced.

Thursday 29 Thanksgiving! Have I anything to give thanks for. I feel that I have—that those at home feel that I am better off than I am. ¶A dreary day of terrible anxiety. Spent it all in my poor lodgings, writing on my tunnel pamphlet, now my last resort. Got over 50 pages, and it is very satisfactory. ¶Went down in the evening, but saw nothing to attract my dejected mind. So returned home (home did I say!) and went to bed, determined to make a big effort to-morrow.

Friday 30 This morning got a title page for the Lake Tunnel pamphlet put in type, and with feelings of great anxiety, went to see Philips, President of the Michigan Southern R. R. He responded nobly, and gave me $75.00 for a card on last page of the cover. Full of renewed hope, called on Dunlap of the Northwestern, and he took a page also. To still further insure the success of the enterprise, Johnson of the Illinois Central did likewise. Went to my lodgings a happier man than for many a day.

Michigan Southern R.R.: The last three pages and the inside and outside of the back cover of the Lake Tunnel pamphlet were full-page ads for railroads. **Dunlap:** See 12/27/65. **Johnson:** W. P. Johnson, general passenger agent of the Illinois Central Railroad.

DECEMBER

Saturday 1 Early at the R.P.P. Association, and put my hastily prepared copy in the hands of the printers. Continued canvassing for advertisements all day, with some success, but enough to ensure the success of this my last straw of hope. ¶At Baker's and ordered an engraving for it, cost $10. ¶In evening received letter from Anna, which relieved me of no little anxiety. She enclosed one from Sheffield, in which he declares they are hard up, and he cannot send me the draft he promised.

R.P.P. Association: Religio-Philosophical Publishing Association, the publishing house W had used for the imprint of his Union Stock Yards pamphlet of 1865. See 12/4/65. **Baker's:** This company had also engraved the map of Union Stock Yard for W's pamphlet the year before. See 12/8/65.

Sunday 2 I remember the Sabbath day to-day, & kept it holy. All day long I wrote on my pamphlet, and at night had the satisfaction of getting almost to the last chapter. ¶Wrote letters to Anna, Sheffield, Jim Creveling, Will Wiggins, etc. ¶All hope grows lighter. The dark clouds begin slowly to disperse, and again Jack Wing catches a dim sight of prosperity through adversity. ¶But will it come?

Monday 3 Again at work on my pamphlet, with poor success in the advertising line. ¶They are getting it along well at the office, and I am now pretty well convinced there is no other in the field. ¶Mailed a letter to Frank Leslie enquiring if I could buy his Lake tunnel electrotypes for the pamphlet. ¶Anxiously awaiting for a letter from Cary with proof of "Dial," but do not get one. He evidently does not care to do printing for me, on that old score.

Frank Leslie: *Frank Leslie's Illustrated Newspaper* had published an article, "The New Chicago Waterworks," on Nov. 3, 1866, pp. 100–101. It includes seven wood engravings of the building of the lake tunnel. **electrotypes:** metal printing plates made from wood engravings.

December 1866

Tuesday 4 With hopeful anticipation of a successful termination of my Lake Tunnel History Project, I keep on working anxiously for it. Refusals to advertise in it at one place only send me flying to another. Read more proof, and hourly see the pamphlet approaching nearer and nearer to a complete thing. ¶Get the engraving from Baker, which is to constitute the frontispiece. ¶Down to Nolan's room in the evening, and make him an offer for half interest in it.

Wednesday 5 Receive a letter from Frank Leslie, stating that he will sell me electrotypes from the Lake Tunnel engravings for 30 cents per square inch. Telegraph him to send the five small ones immediately. ¶Walsh, who refused to have anything to do with my Stock Yard pamphlet, agrees to take the agency for this, and also to send advanced proof sheets to New York and other dailies. ¶So here is a little more hope! ¶Wait! Jack! Wait!

five small ones: The two W did not buy were large panoramic views, which would have added considerably to the cost of the pamphlet.
Walsh: John R. Walsh was born in 1837 in Ireland and migrated to the U.S. and Chicago in 1849. He was president of the Western News Company on the corner of Dearborn and Madison and was the biggest newspaper distributor in the midwest throughout the Civil War. His company distributed half the total copies of both the *Tribune* and *Times*. Walsh also took an ad in the tunnel pamphlet.

Thursday 6 More unsuccessful week canvassing, & more proof reading. ¶If there be any one drawback to my success in anything, it is that I am too impatient—too nervous—to abide results. Every hour that passes, now seems an age, for I am all eager expectation. Whenever the chances of a failure arise, they seem to entirely darken my horizon. ¶But I believe I am not all unworthy of success! One thing is now certain, my wild oats are sown.

more proof reading: The lake tunnel was officially inaugurated this day, although it would be more than three months before water from it was delivered throughout the city. W describes the ceremony in his pamphlet but obviously was not there. He most likely got the account from friends or newspaper reports.

Friday 7 Made an arrangement with Tobin (a jeweller[)], to give him half a page in pamphlet, pay him $15, and receive a music box which he has. If I get a room, and can spare the money, this will be a great pleasure to one so universally alone as I, yet ever so fond of society. ¶Work on pamphlet still progresses. Called on Chesbrough, and showed him my enterprise. Receive little or no encouragement. ¶Dark, rainy and terribly muddy. Did not leave my lodgings in the evening.

Tobin: Benjamin F. Tobin ran the Eagle Jewelry Store on the corner of Clark and Madison streets. **Chesbrough:** Ellis S. Chesbrough (1813–86), engineer of the Chicago Board of Public Works, proposed the original idea of creating a lake tunnel to provide the city with fresh drinking water.

Saturday 8 Talked with Caryl Young in the morning about starting a skating paper, but he does not seem to favor it. ¶Recd "No" from the C.B. & Q.R.R. ¶Got an Adv for cover from Maynard Bros, and in return get $15, a night lock, and a splendid rifle. Better than nothing. ¶In the afternoon Foster of my old building, offered to rent me a neat little room for $8.00 per month, and I agreed to take. ¶Looked at some carpeting, down to Nolan's.

Caryl Young: W had met him at the beginning of the year on 1/3/66. **C.B. & Q.R.R.:** Chicago, Burlington & Quincy Railroad. **Maynard Bros.:** The Maynard Brothers, who sold safes and locks from their store at 47 State Street, had an advertisement on the inside of the front cover of the tunnel pamphlet. **my old building:** Tyler's Block. See 10/18/65.

Sunday 9 Sunday! My second in Chicago, since the return of the "Prodigal Son." ¶Spent the entire day in my poor lodgings, reading and writing. It was long, O, how long, and rendered doubly so by the terrible anxiety of mind I am in. ¶Down to Nolan's room in evening. Met a merry party of boys there, and had a pleasant time, enjoying the relief from "brooding cares" very much. Stayed out until midnight—a very unusual thing for me now. I have sown my wild oats.

Monday 10 A bitter cold day. Anxiously looking for my cuts from Frank Leslie, but they do not come. Am afraid I shall be badly bothered with them. ¶Canvassed for advs with poor success. Finally run against a fellow who will take half a page, and let it go on a bill of furniture, and whom I can get a pretty good bargain on a carpet. ¶Got a cool box up into my room. ¶Recd letters from Anna, Sate Hinman, Leonard YB, and package of posters from Cary.

half a page: A half-page ad for John B. Walsh Wholesale Dealer in Furniture and Chairs appeared in the tunnel pamphlet. Walsh's store was at 100 Madison Street, "three doors west of Dearborn." **cool box:** likely some sort of food storage container. **posters:** advertising posters for the Lake Tunnel pamphlet?

Tuesday 11 A long day of anxious waiting. After making a tour of all the express offices, I learned that my cuts have not come, from some unaccountable reason. ¶Anything but this horrible waiting for something to come, upon which depends almost my very existence, and not have it come. It is worse than the tortures of the rack. ¶Neither does Walsh hear from the sample copies of the Tunnel pamphlet, which he sent nearly a week ago.

sample copies: See 12/5/66, when Walsh agreed to send proof sheets to New York. All the ads, other than those appearing on the inside of the front and back cover, were printed following the text so that the pamphlet could be published without the illustrations.

Wednesday 12 Got up from my straw pallet at the Lloyd House (my retreat in poverty) with the expression on my lips—"I hope they will come to-day.["] *But they did not come.* ¶In the afternoon telegraphed to Frank Leslie, in almost a fit of desperation. But as if to add to my awful torment, do not even get an answer to the dispatch. ¶When one has no place to rest the sole of his foot, that he may call his own, there is nothing more terrible than waiting.

straw pallet: It is hard to say whether W is being hyperbolic here or whether he was indeed sleeping on a straw pallet. The Lloyd House, situated south of the main downtown center at Polk and Clark streets, was a cheap hotel. See 8/28/65 for W's earlier stay at the Lloyd House.

Thursday 13 No electrotypes, and no answer to my dispatch. ¶Got the carpet down on my room floor, and "shoved-up" my precious diamond ring for $50.00 to pay for it. But that is all right, as the carpet is a big trade. ¶In the evening, very late, received a dispatch, directed to "J. R. Wing", from Frank Leslie, stating that the "cuts were delayed by accident, but that he would forward [them] Friday." Even this is better than sas-pense. Decided to wait for them and to go to Waukegan to kill time to-morrow.

Friday 14 Hastened and up walked to depot for Waukegan. Arrived there, and shipped my dear old books back to the same building they left a year ago. This is the return of the prodigal son. ¶Got through the day rather pleasantly with Loveridge who is something of a genius in his way; and a very strange character withal. Cary will not print the Dial—says he has not got "sorts." ¶Returned to my Lloyd House wallowing in the mire.

"sorts": printing type of a particular size and style.

Saturday 15 Another day of waiting. ¶My dear old books arrived, and I carried them all up stairs to my room, or rather the commencement of my room, that is to be. ¶Feel great anxiety because I cannot send money to Anna before my cuts come. But it will be better late than never. ¶Fell in with a country boy at Lloyd House in evening (Frank Edwards) whom I entertain and get acquainted with. A Fair sort of a fellow.

Sunday 16 A long day of anxious doubts and fears. Very stormy, the first snow of the season, drifting, and a prospect that all the railroads are blocked up, and that my long expected, long delayed express package will not get through in some time yet. ¶Stayed in doors all day, and in the evening, needing exercise, went down to the old building where my room is, and stayed a few hours with Nolan and Franklin. Then back to the Lloyd House, and went to bed.

Franklin: Perhaps Alonzo Franklin, a teller at the Merchants, Farmers and Mechanics' Savings Bank, who lived down the street from Tyler's Block at 86 LaSalle.

Monday 17 A rough day. In the morning delayed going down as long as possible, in hopes that I *would* find my package when I did go. Then went down only to meet with the same disappointment. Decided that if the cuts did not come by to-morrow noon, that I would get out the book without them. Got an advanced copy, and it looks pretty well. ¶In the evening stopped in doors in my poor lodgings at that seat of my poverty—the Lloyd House.

advanced copy: The five pages containing the illustrations were later glued into the pamphlet. There are no known copies of the pamphlet without the illustrations.

Tuesday 18 In the morning determined to get a stove up in my room, and did—total cost $26.00. On going to the Printers surprised to learn that my "cuts" had at last come, C.O.D. $34.75, but that the messenger had carried them off again. How to raise money to pay for them was now the question. But I succeeded in getting $75.00 from the NWRR. While looking for cuts at MU Ex Co. in afternoon, run against Lon Kenyon & Joe Quimby, a YB. It quite upset me. We all went on a spree at my expense, at opera in eve.

NWRR: Northwestern Railroad. **MU Ex Co.:** Merchants' Union Express Company at Dearborn and Washington streets. **opera:** The Bateman Concert was performing a musical program of songs, arias, and piano pieces at Crosby's.

Wednesday 19 Awoke to find myself at the old Briggs House, the worse for wear and about $25 out of pocket. Had got my cuts last night, while tight, & taken them to the office. ¶Dined at Briggs with the boys, and in afternoon, we all went riding over to the tunnel, which we went into, and also riding on the avenues. Got a copy of my book with cuts in all right, and gave to the boys, and left them bound for old Oswego & Syracuse, at the Briggs House.

Thursday 20 Collecting in the morning, with fair success. Got all of my furniture into my room, paid the balance on it, $88.50, and got down my trunk from the Lloyd House. In the evening carried copies of pamphlet to the Times, Tribune & Republican, and also 50 to Walsh. ¶Got into my room in the evening, borrowed coal, and got a fire. It is dear little place—the best I ever had in my life. Three times and out for me, on rooms. Never more tired in my life.

Three times and out: A baseball convention was currently being held at the Briggs House and may have inspired W's metaphor.

Friday 21 Up by sunrise, and rush for the morning papers. The *Republican* alone notices my book, and that very favorably. The Bohemians have gone back on me. Well, I have accomplished my object—*got me a home again.* ¶Spent the day in delivering books around to the different stores, and in collecting my bills. Spent the evening in my nobly room, feeling much better than in a long time before. Got my rifle from Maynards, & my night lock for my door.

The *Republican* alone notices my book: A brief review of *The Great Chicago Tunnel* appeared in *The Republican* on page 8, column 1. **The Bohemians:** See 9/10/65.

Saturday 22 The Tribune Bohemians manifest their hatred of me by a very sarcastic notice of my pamphlet. It is entirely characteristic of the sheet. ¶Went to the tunnel in the morning, and carried over 50 pamphlets. Sold two of them for 50 cents each while there, & left the rest on sale. Heard on my way back that Walsh has gone back on me, but can learn nothing of it by going there. ¶In evening got Geo. Armstrong, my Col Bowen friend to stay with me. A bully boy.

a very sarcastic notice: The *Tribune* notice appeared on page 4, column 1. Although this mention was shorter than the one in the *Republican,* it hardly seems sarcastic: "A very remarkable sketch of the lake tunnel, from its inception to its conclusion, has been compiled by Jack Wing, and is just issued by the Western News Company of this city. It is copiously illustrated." **Geo. Armstrong:** The city directory lists him as an "usher" (i.e., a doorman) at Bowen Bros. **Col Bowen:** See 1/17/66.

Sunday 23 At home! ¶Once more can I say that I have a home. And it is the best one I have ever known, since I left that one so far away, and yet so dear—notwithstanding its poverty. Yes, in my own cosy room, I feel the dear enjoyment of *home.* ¶Read and wrote all day, enjoying it well. My music box (got from an Adv in pamphlet of tunnel) is quite an enlivener of my solitude. ¶And thus am I back again in this dear old building.

At home!: W has returned to a room in the LaSalle Street building (Tyler's Block), where he had lived before he left Chicago the previous April. See 12/8/66.

Cross section of the digging of the lake tunnel. This frontispiece to *The Great Chicago Lake Tunnel,* made by Baker's Engraving House, is closely based on one of the illustrations for W's front-page *Times* article on the tunnel published on July 25, 1865.

Monday 24 After breakfast at the restaurant, went down to M.C.R.R. with pamphlets. Sargeant paid my bill, and also ordered 20 copies for $5. Collected my bill of MCNally, and several others. Met Col Binmore in afternoon, and paid him $5 as my dues to the Bohemian Club. Also settled my long standing bill at Bamford & Baldwin, by letting them have some pamphlets. ¶Called on Lib Williams in the evening, and had a pleasant talk.

Sargeant: Homer E. Sargeant, general freight agent for the Michigan Central Railroad. **20 copies for $5:** The wholesale price of the pamphlet was twenty-five cents each. **MCNally:** John McNally & Co., a bookseller at 81 Dearborn Street. **Col Binmore:** See 4/4/66. **Bamford & Baldwin:** booksellers. See 9/8/65. **Lib Williams:** childhood friend from the late 1850s in Pulaski, N.Y. Surprisingly, this is the first mention of seeing her in Chicago.

Tuesday 25 Christmas! ¶A beautiful day, but no snow. After dinner met Barathy & Willy Meneer, who went to my room. I joined them at the rink in evening, and there met Clark, an old geneva "Sig." Others soon joined the party and we had several "Tom & Jerrys," separating at a late hour. ¶Willy M. (whom I have long longed to know) went home with me, and we had a very pleasant night. I fear that the son of wealth has stolen my best affections.

geneva "Sig": member of a YB chapter in Geneva, N.Y. **"Tom & Jerrys":** a drink made with rum, hot sweetened water, and spices. **Barathy & Willy Meneer:** untraced.

Wednesday 26 This morning, after taking Meneer with me to breakfast, took him down to the tunnel, and we went out as far as the first chamber. ¶Tried to get a settlement with old Walsh in the afternoon, but could not. He has used me d—d mean to say the least. Collected my bill, and $3.00 more of R. J. Walsh, who is one of the whitest men in Chicago. In my room in the evening reading the January "Galaxy."

old Walsh: John R. Walsh, news agent. See 12/5/66. **R. J. Walsh:** Robert J. Walshe, the tailor, had taken an ad in the Lake Tunnel pamphlet. See 10/2/66. **whitest:** fairest, most honest. **"Galaxy":** *The Galaxy,* "A Magazine of entertaining reading," began in May 1866 and would merge with *The Atlantic* in 1878. The issue W was reading contained the first part of "Tristan" by Edward Spencer, chapter 36 of Anthony Trollope's "The Claverings," and other pieces of prose and poetry.

Thursday 27 An intensely bitter cold day. Got up very late, and breakfasted on cakes and coffee. The fire in my room would not burn, and I got froze out. ¶In the afternoon over to R P P Association, and drew out a diagram for THE DIAL, also got figures on the frames, at Cross, Dane & Westlakes. ¶In the evening Franklin came up and had a pipe with me. Went over to Brunswicks, but could not find anybody. At Walshes and got a "big" Diary for next year.

a diagram for THE DIAL: probably a page layout. This publication never appeared. **the frames:** Stands to support type cases. This curious technical reference may suggest that W was thinking of setting *The Dial* himself. **Cross, Dane & Westlakes:** stove and hollow ware wholesalers. From the context, it would appear they also handled printing paraphernalia. **Diary:** An 1867 diary, if ever begun, has not survived.

Friday 28 Fire out in the morning, and the cold intense. Built it, and did my "house work." ¶Over to the tunnel in the afternoon, & found that but few of my books had been sold, and poor prospect of any being sold there. ¶Ordered 50 contracts for advertising in the next edition of the pamphlet, which I have decided to get out. ¶Up to the Lloyd House in the evening, and got a letter from Anna. Wrote her, & enclosed a dollar.

the next edition: W did produce a second, longer edition (eighty pages as compared with sixty-four pages) of the Lake Tunnel pamphlet with many more advertisements. Like the Union Stock Yards pamphlet, it was probably produced in January or February of 1867, since W was already taking ads for it. Both editions bear a publishing date of 1867, but the second edition contains the words "Special Edition" on the cover. A third illustrated "Hotel edition" was published in 1868, either prior to W's departure for Europe in March of that year, or after his return in August.

Saturday 29 Walsh (Western News Co) settled with me this morning, for what books he had had, and I received a small pittance of $15. ¶Bought a splendid bookcase at Gilbert & Sampsons for $25, and put my books into it in afternoon. ¶In evening thought I would call upon Bob Arthur, an Alpha YB in town. Found that he had been hunting for me. Called on him—a magnificent home on Wabash Av. He came down and stayed with me all night.

a small pittance: If W had wholesaled the pamphlet to Walsh at twenty-five cents each, $15 would represent the sale of sixty books in ten days. **Bob Arthur:** possibly a son or relative of William Robert Arthur, general superintendent of the Illinois Central Railroad, who lived at 578 Wabash.

Sunday 30 Took Arthur, the favored child of Fortune, down to breakfast, after which he went home. ¶Arranged my room (I am my own housekeeper, & am mighty well pleased with my arrangements) made my toillette read THE TIMES, and wrote letters to Bill Wiggins, Jim Creveling, Leonard Kenyon and Sallie Curtiss. ¶Bob Arthur up in room again in the afternoon, bringing a friend with him. ¶Boynton of BF & Co up in room in eve. A good chat with him.

Leonard Kenyon: usually referred to as Lon Kenyon in the diaries. See, for example, 12/18/66, when W runs into him in Chicago. **Sallie Curtiss:** a relative on W's mother's side of the family. **Boynton:** Charles W. Boynton, partner of Boynton, Foster & Co., commission merchants and advertisers in the Lake Tunnel pamphlet.

Monday 31 Over to Tourtelott's in morning, but met a wizzen-face, spectacled advertising man already there, & did not broach the subject of my call. Recd the usual "No" from Richards. ¶In the afternoon received some encouragement from Fuller, Finch & Fuller, & also from Foster, at Fairbanks & Greenleafs. ¶New Years eve. After supper sallied forth but did not succeed in finding anybody that I knew or cared to talk with, and so went back to my room and went to bed.

[At the bottom of the page] over

Tourtelott's: Tourtelot Brothers, manufacturers of Tourtelot's Extract of Beef, and preserved meats, game, fish, soups, etc. They did advertise in the second edition of the Lake Tunnel pamphlet. **Richards:** A likely candidate is Joshua C. Richards, general superintendent of Richards' Corn Sheller Works. **Fuller, Finch & Fuller:** Oliver F. Fuller, Chicago partner of a company of importers and wholesalers of drugs and medicines. They took a full-page ad in the second edition of the Lake Tunnel pamphlet. **Fairbanks & Greenleafs:** See 12/28/65.

Memorandum

Another year is dead, and another volume of this veracious history of my erratic daily life finished. It is well!

It were worse than vain to recapitulate the scenes I have passed through in the year just closed. It's advent found me in the *Republican* office, and shortly after witnessed my ejectment from there. Then followed the sucessful pamphlet on the Stock Yards, my lonely days without anything to do, etc. Then in rapid succession comes my Waukegan *fiasco,* and its train of horrors, my doleful journey home etc; my return to Detroit, the Post *emute,* my arrival almost penniless again in the Garden City, my departure for the Crescent City, arrival there and fruitless sojourn and adventures, my voyage up the Father of Waters, and consequent meeting with the Rogers party of Boston (the most pleasant feature of my life) my Advent in St Louis, the baneful partnership of S. W. & Co. and all that followed; its unhappy termination, my pleasant journey east, visit to the hub and N.Y. my third return to Chicago, and the struggles which I again encountered, and their results.

It is in detail recorded these pages, and cursed be the man

who shall think harshly of me and my career when he reads these pages.

And so I part with 1866, with less of compunction of conscience for the past, than of hopes of a bright future.

emute: W's misspelling of *émeute,* French for a riot or disturbance. Once again W shows a rather bizzare comprehension of French. **Crescent City**: New Orleans. **Rogers party**: C. O. Rogers, owner of the *Boston Journal,* and his son, Charles, whom W had met April 22, on his return journey from New Orleans. W had visited the Rogerses in Boston in November of this year and would travel to Europe with the younger Rogers from March to August of 1868 as overseas correspondent for the *Journal,* writing travel articles during this "grand tour." **S. W. & Co.**: Sheffield, Wing & Co. Advertising Agency in St. Louis where W was a partner from May 3 to October 26, 1866. **hub**: Boston. **N.Y.**: New York City. W visited there on November 20 and 21.

Appendixes
References
Index

Appendix A: Descriptions of the Diaries

1865

13.5 x 8.2 cm.

Imitation black diced leather cover. Flap from back cover extending over fore edge and tucking into a strip laced into front cover. Double rule blind stamped on front and back cover and the irregularly shaped flap. Spine stamped in gold "Diary of John M. Wing 1865" in roman upper- and lowercase letters. Flap stamped in gold "DIARY 1865" in sans serif roman capitals.

All edges gilt. Tube for pencil inside flap fore edge.

The front pastedown carries an Old Corner Library bookplate with 2586 stamped in red in the upper-left corner.

Recto of front flyleaf (in ink): VOL. VIII. | [Rule] | J. M. Wing, [cypher] YB.,| Utica Morning Herald | and | Oswego Com'l Advertiser | & Times | [Rule] | and | Chicago Daily Times | and | Chicago Republican

Title page: Thick-thin ruled border. DIARY | POCKET | REMEMBRANCER | FOR | 1865. | [Two rules with facing arrowheads separated by a solid bullet] | FOR THE TRADE

Verso of title page: Calendar for 1865

Front matter: Postage rates on following recto & verso.

One page for each day of the year.

Memorandum of 7 pages.

Contents of wallet in back of diary: A lock of brown hair. A pass for the Northern Transportation Company for 1865, 5.5 x 9.3 cm, printed in blue and red, made out to "J. M. Wing Esq. | Local Editor, "Oswego | Coml Advertiser" and signed by "P. Chamberlin, Prest." Verso list the names of fifteen screw steamers owned by the company and terms of the free ticket.

1866

16.5 x 10.5 cm.

Quarter imitation black leather with grain textured black cloth sides. Front cover stamped in gold ornamental capitals DAILY | JOURNAL | 1866, with a leaf decoration springing from "J." Spine stamped "Diary of John M. Wing 1866" as on 1865 diary.

All edges marbled.

Appendix A Front pastedown carries Old Corner Library bookplate with 2587 stamped in red in the upper-left corner.

Flyleaf: Jack Wing | THE CHICAGO REPUBLICAN |[below in pale ink] Sheffield, Wing & Co's | Advertising Agency | 47, North Fourth St | St Louis, Mo. | [Pen flourish]

Title page: Thick-thin ruled border with typographic ornaments in the corners. [In manuscript] Jack Wing | [Type] DAILY JOURNAL | FOR | 1866. | [Typographic ornament] | PUBLISHED ANNUALLY | [black letter type] for the Trade. | [roman type] MDCCCLXVI.

Page ii: blank

Page iii: Counting House Calendar | 1866.

One page for each day of the year.

Memorandum of three pages.

Back pastedown: Newspaper clippings from the *Pulaski Democrat* and the *Rome Sentinel* announcing W's partnership in the *Waukegan Gazette.* Photo of J. H. Emerick with "The Last One" written below in W's hand. Emerick was a friend killed in the Civil War.

No wallet inside back cover.

Appendix B: 1865–66 Chicago Publications of John M. Wing, Including His Newspaper Articles

This bibliography of the Chicago writings of John M. Wing published during 1865 and 1866 is based on his diary entries. The *Tribune* and *Times* consisted of a single folded sheet of four unnumbered pages of eight columns each. The *Republican* had eight numbered pages of six columns each. For ease of reference, I have numbered the *Tribune* and *Times* pages as follows: front cover, p. 1; verso of front, p. 2; recto of back page p. 3; back page, p. 4. Column numbers are from left to right. Some articles are preceded by several lines of headlines, for which I give the first few lines when they need amplification.

CHICAGO TRIBUNE, 1865

6/7 The Law Courts. p. 4, col. 3.
6/7 The Opera. p. 4, col. 4.

CHICAGO TIMES, 1865

6/9 The Late Disastrous Fire. p. 3, cols 3 & 4.
6/12 The City. The Heroes . . . Arrival of the Lieutenant General. p. 3, cols 1 & 2.
6/13 The Returning Veterans. Great Dissatisfaction at Camp Fry . . . p. 3, col. 1.
6/13 The Schools. p. 3, col. 3.
6/15 The Courts. p. 3, col. 3.
6/16 The Courts. p. 3, col. 5.
6/17 A Disastrous Fire. p. 3, col. 3.
6/17 The Returning Troops. | Arrival of Hecker Regiment . . . p. 3, cols 2 & 3.
6/18 Gen. Sherman. His Movements. p. 3, col. 6.
6/18 The Crosby Testimonial. p. 3, col. 7.
6/20 The City. A Terrific Explosion. p. 2, col. 6
6/20 Ovation to the Hecker Regiment. p. 2, cols 6 & 7.
6/21 The City. The Fair. *s.v.* The Receipts. p. 3, col. 1.
6/21 The Tug-Boat Explosion. p. 2, col. 5.
6/23 Lager on the Decline. p. 3, col. 3.
6/24 The University of Notre Dame.| Interesting Anniversary Exercises. p. 1, cols 4– 6.
6/27 The Late Storm. Extraordinary Violence—A Grand Carnival of the Elements—Freaks of the Lightning. p. 3, col. 1.

6/27 Seduction. A Distressing Case of Recent Occurrence. p. 3, cols 1 & 2
6/28 University of St. Mary's of the Lake. Nineteenth Annual Commencement. p. 3, col. 3.
6/28 Immigration. Great Rush to the West. p. 3, col. 4.
6/28 On the River. p. 3, cols 4 & 5.
6/29 Early Fruit. Some Interesting Facts. p. 2, col. 8.
6/29 The Courts. p. 3, col. 2.
6/29 The Mammoth Crib. p. 3, col. 2.
6/30 The Tricks of Trade. Contemptible Devices of Designing Shop-Keepers. p. 3, col. 4.
7/1 The Murderer's Doom. The Execution of William Bell at Waukegan. A Graphic Account by Our Special Reporter. p. 2, cols 6–8: p. 3, col. 1.
7/3 Military Movements. Arrival of the 92d Illinois Regiment. p. 3, col. 2.
7/4 The Returning Veterans. Arrival of Battery A. p. 2, col. 8.
7/4 Police Court. p. 3, col. 2
7/6 Bell, The Murderer . . . Further Developments—An Intimation of Guilt—Partial Confession—Meeting of Spiritualists. p. 2, col. 2.
7/6 Board of Education. p. 2, col. 3.
7/7 Behind Bars. The Jail and its Inmates. Demireps in Prison—p. 3, col. 2.
7/7 Public Parks. Summer Discomforts and How to Remove Them. p. 3, col. 3.
7/7 Much Ado about Nothing. p. 3, col. 4.
7/10 A Gipsy Encampment. Fortune-Tellers and Chicken-Stealers. p. 3, cols 1 & 2.
7/10 Our Fallen Heroes. Monuments to their Memory. p. 3, col. 2.
7/10 Military Movements. Arrival of the 57th Illinois Regiment. p. 3, col.. 3.
7/11 A Shocking Incident. A Child Dies in its Mother's Arms. p. 2, col. 7.
7/14 The Dearborn Street Tragedy. Impertinent and Revolting Curiosity. p. 3, col. 3.
7/17 The City. The Thieves of Chicago. Museum of Stolen Goods. p. 3, col. 1.
7/17 The Public Schools. Special Meeting of the Board of Education. p. 3, col. 2.
7/17 Summer Recreation. The Annual Hegira to the Watering Places. p. 3, col. 4.
7/18 Frightful Accident. Fatal Walk by Somnambulist. p. 3, col. 1.
7/19 On the Streets. Glimpse into Shop Windows—. p. 3, col. 1.
7/19 An Indigo Bath. How Green Became Blue by Missing the Right Tank. p. 3, col. 2.
7/19 Crim. Con. The Transgression of War-Widows. p. 3, col. 3.
7/20 An Important Sanitary Reform. The Removal of Garbage. p. 2, col. 8.
7/20 The Gift Enterprise. Trial and Conviction of Several Proprietors. p. 3, col. 2.
7/22 The City. Scenes of Terror. A Frightful Riot in the North Division. p. 2, cols 7 & 8.

7/24	Petty Feuds. Disgraceful Finale of the Sanitary Fair. p. 3, col. 2.
7/24	Raid on the Gamblers. A Rural Assemblage—Over One Hundred Captured—. p. 3, cols 3 & 4.
7/24	Flies! Flies! Flies! p. 3, col. 5.
7/25	The Great Lake Tunnel. The Successful Launch of the Crib. [As W mentions, this article contained an illustration, something rare for the *Times*.] p. 1, cols 4–7.
7/25	A Murderer Arrested. He is "Pulled" in the Great Sunday Raid, and Recognized in Court by the Detectives. [This seems a likely candidate for the "sensation article" mentioned by W on 7/24.] p. 3, col. 1.
7/26	Further Concerning the Doings of Don Juan de Casta. p. 3, col. 5.
7/27	The Rush to Chicago. Hundreds of Young Men out of Employment. p. 3, col. 2.
7/27	Negro Immigration. p. 3, col. 3.
7/29	"Who Pays the Drinks?" p. 3, col. 2.
7/29	Proposed Jaunt of The City Government. [Possibly one of the "several items . . . suggested by the meeting of the common council. . . ." mentioned by W on 7/28.] p. 3, col. 2.
7/29	Our Toronto Visitor. [Possibly one of the "several items . . . suggested by the meeting of the common council" mentioned by W on 7/28.] p. 3, col. 2.
7/31	The City. On 'Change. Exciting Scenes Among the Grain Operators. p. 3, col. 2.
7/31	Our Amusements . . . Italian Opera More Liberally Sustained in Chicago than in New York. p. 3, col. 3.
8/2	A Dusky Occasion. Anniversary of Emancipation in the West Indies. p. 3, col. 2.
8/2	Professional Thieves. Glimpses Inside the Ring. p. 3, col. 3.
8/3	The City. Lake View Avenue Drive. p. 2, col. 7.
8/3	Excitement on Wells Street. Another Great Raid by Police. p. 2, col. 7.
8/4	The City . . . The Homeward March. p. 3, col. 1.
8/4	The German Musical Societies. An Interesting Event. p. 3, col. 2.
8/4	Great Raid upon Cattle. p. 3, col. 2.
8/7	The Army and Navy. Organization of a United Service Club. p. 2, cols 2 & 3.
8/7	The City. Squatter Settlements. Shanty Life in Chicago. p. 3, cols 1 & 2.
8/7	To Be Tried for His Life. p. 3, col. 3.
8/12	A Terrible Tornado. Great Destruction of Property at South Bend, Ind. p. 2, col. 7.
8/12	The City. | The Three Golden Balls. Pawnbroker's Shops and their History . . . p. 3, col. 1.
8/14	The Progress of Chicago . . . Halpin's City Directory. p. 1, cols 4–6.
8/16	Gen. Grant. [Telegraph reports from Detroit, Dearborn, Ypsilanti, Ann Arbor, Jackson, "On Board," Albion, Marshall, and Kalamazoo, Mich.] p. 2, cols 3 & 4.
8/16	From Detroit. p. 2, col. 5.

8/17 The City. Gen. Grant . . . The Arrival in Chicago. p. 2, col. 8.
8/17 The Lake Tunnel An Illustrious Party Visit the Works. p. 3, col. 1.
8/18 From Michigan City, Ind. The Harbor Convention. p. 2, cols 4 & 5.
8/19 The Latest by Telegraph. Movements of Gen. Grant. p. 2, cols 4 & 5.
8/22 A Deserted Wife. | Husband Abandons his Spouse on a Railroad Train—Frantic Actions of the Woman. p. 3, col. 1.
8/23 The City. Terrible Marine Disaster. p. 3, col. 1.
8/23 A Terrible Accident. A Boy Run Over and his Head Crushed. p. 3, col. 3.
8/24 Great Camp Meeting The Methodists Encamped at Desploines [*sic*] Grove. p. 3, cols 2 & 3.
8/24 A Horrible Affair. Dreadful Death from an Attempt to Procure an Abortion. [Partly by W. See his entry for 8/23.] p. 3, col. 1.
8/26 Home Gossip. | The Street Musicians of Chicago. p. 3, col. 2.
8/28 The City. | The Chicago River. p. 3, cols 1–3.
8/31 The New Chamber of Commerce. | Inaugural Ceremonies Yesterday. p. 4, cols 1–8.
9/1 The City. The Chamber of Commerce. p. 2, cols 1–3.
9/4 The City. The State Fair. p. 3, cols 1 & 2.
9/6 The City. The State Fair. p. 2, col. 8; p. 3, cols 1 & 2.
9/7 The City. The State Fair. p. 2, col. 8; p. 3, cols 1–3.
9/8 The City. The State Fair. p. 2, cols 7 & 8; p. 3, cols 1–3.
9/11 The City. The State Fair . . . The Closing Day. p. 3, cols 3 & 4.
9/12 From Galena. Gen. Grant's Excursion to Covington, Ky. [Not mentioned by W but a telegraph dispatch from Galena while he was there.] p. 2, col. 4.
9/13 The Latest by Telegraph . . . The Excursion of Gen. Grant. p. 2, cols 5 & 6.
9/14 The Latest by Telegraph . . . Gen. Grant's Excursion. p. 2, cols 4 & 5.
9/15 The Latest by Telegraph . . . The English Railway Capitalist. p. 2, col. 3.
9/15 The Latest by Telegraph . . . Gen. Grant. | His Movements. p. 2, cols 3 & 4.
9/18 American Union Commission. Proceedings of the Meeting Last Evening. p. 3, cols 6 & 7
9/21 The Latest by Telegraph . . . Michigan State Fair. p. 2, cols 4 & 5.
9/22 The Latest by Telegraph . . . Michigan State Fair. p. 2, cols 4 & 5.
9/23 The Latest by Telegraph . . . Close of the Michigan State Fair. p. 2, col. 4.
9/27 The Latest by Telegraph . . . From Janesville, Wis. The Radical Republican Convention. The State Fair. p. 2, col. 5.
9/28 The Times. By Telegraph. The Wisconsin Radical Convention . . . Wisconsin State Fair. p. 2, cols 3 & 4.

9/29 The Latest by Telegraph. The Wisconsin Radical Convention. p. 2, cols 3–5.
9/30 The Latest by Telegraph. The Wisconsin State Fair Address of Gen. Sherman. p. 2, cols 3 & 4.
10/2 Rowina Gambling Hell . . . The Notorious Capt. Hyman the Principal Actor in the Scene. p. 3, cols 2 & 3.
10/5 The Latest by Telegraph . . . Indiana State Fair. p. 2, cols 5 & 6.
10/5 "Arrival of Secretary McCulloch." Special Dispatch Fort Wayne. [Not mentioned by W but reported from Ft. Wayne while he was there.] p. 2, col. 6.
10/7 The Latest by Telegraph . . . "From Fort Wayne, Ind." p. 2, cols 4–6.
10/9 The Latest by Telegraph . . . "From Fort Wayne, Ind." p. 2, cols 4 & 5.
10/11 The City. Our Postoffice. p. 3, col. 1.
10/11 Gossip for Gentlemen. p. 3, col. 1.
10/12 The City. | Subjects for Charity . . . Concerning Coal Dealers. p. 3, col. 1.
10/12 Too Much of a Good Thing. p. 3, col. 3.
10/16 Sporting Matters. The Turf, Base-Ball and Cricket. [W wrote the report on the turf.] p. 3, col. 5.
10/17 The City. A Destructive Conflagration. p. 3, cols 1 & 2.
10/18 The Coal Question. p. 3, col. 2.
10/19 The Boston Lancers. p. 3, col. 2.
10/20 The City. The Boston Lancers. p. 3, cols 1 & 2.
10/20 The Eclipse. p. 3, col. 2.
10/21 The City. Our Eastern Visitors. p. 3, cols 1–4.
10/23 The Orphans' Fair. p. 3, col. 2.
10/25 An Appalling Leap. p. 3, col. 2.
10/26 Local Politics. The Cook County Republican Convention. p. 3, cols 1 & 2.
10/27 The City. The Republican County Convention. p. 3, cols 1–3.
10/28 An Indignation Meeting. Republicans Denouncing the Hesing Ticket. p. 3, col. 2.
10/30 The City. Local Politics. Great Excitement among the Republicans. p. 3, cols 1–3.
10/30 Highly Important to Voters. The Registry Law. p. 3, cols 3 & 4.
10/31 The Registry Law. Where and When to Register. p. 4, col. 3. [This is more "statistical" than the article of 10/30. In it are listed all the wards and districts in Chicago.]
11/2 Artesian Wells. Another Well Completed in Chicago. p. 1, cols 4 & 5.
11/3 A Singular Personage. "The Great American Traveler." . . . A Crazy Diogenes in Pursuit of Fame. p. 3, cols 3 & 4.
11/4 The City. Local Politics. Enthusiasm for the Soldiers' Ticket. [Possibly by W] p. 3, col. 2.
11/6 The Protestant Episcopal Church . . . Sermon Last Evening by the Right Rev. Dr. Clarkson, Bishop Elect of Nebraska and Dakota. p. 3, cols 1 & 2.
11/8 The Election. p. 3, cols 1–3.
11/30 The Lake Tunnel. Progress of the Undertaking. p. 3, cols 1 & 2.
12/1 Saint Andrew. Historical Reminiscences of the Day. Commemorative Festivities. p. 3, cols 1–4.

CHICAGO REPUBLICAN, 1865–1866

12/13 The Commerce of Chicago The List of Our Lake Craft. p. 4, cols 4–6.

12/16 The Murderers' Doom Execution of Corbett and Fleming. p. 2, cols 4–6; p. 3, cols 1–3.

12/17 Heavy Fire in South Water St. Business Block Burned. p. 2, col. 3.

12/18 Sunday in the Churches. A Sermon by the Rev. W. H. Ryder. p. 2, cols 2–5. [This is the entire sermon and is preceded by a short introduction. When W writes "Got Dr. Ryder's sermon in the evening" I assume he means he obtained a transcript of it rather than took it down verbatim.]

12/19 Police Reports. p. 2, col. 5.

12/20 Police Reports. p. 2, col. 3.

12/21 Fires A Barn and Eight Horses Destroyed. p. 2, col. 2. [? There was no Police Report in the paper this day. This local item might have been reported by W.]

12/22 Police Reports. p. 2, col. 4.

12/23 Police Reports. p. 2, col. 3.

12/30 Police Reports. p. 2, col. 3.

1/1 Chicago in 1865 . . . Trade and Commerce. p. 3, cols 4–6.

1/2 The Union Stock Yards. p. 8, cols 1–3.

1/4 The Skating Last Evening**.** First Appearance of Miss Carrie A. Moore. p. 2, cols 3 & 4.

1/5 Police Reports. p. 2, col. 3.

THE RELIGIO-PHILOSOPHICAL PUBLISHING ASSOCIATION, 1865–1866

12/13 Jack Wing. *The Great Union Stock Yards of Chicago.* 1865. Frontispiece + 32 pp. + 10 pp. of advertising.

ca. 1/15 ———. *The Great Union Stock Yards of Chicago.* "Printed by the Religio-Philosophical Publishing Association." 1866. Frontispiece + 32 pp. + 12 pp. of advertising.

J. M. WING & CO., 1866–1867

12/19 John M. Wing. *The Great Chicago Lake Tunnel.* 1867. Frontispiece + 56 pp. + 8 pp. of advertising. [Although this edition carries an 1867 date, the relevant diary entries indicate it was published in 1866.]

?/? ———. *The Great Chicago Lake Tunnel.* 1867. Frontispiece + 80 pp. + 28 1/2 pp. of advertising within the text pages. [This edition carries the same year of publication as the first edition. If W followed the procedure he used for the Stock Yards pamphlet, this edition of the Lake Tunnel booklet may have been published early in 1867.]

Appendix C: "Squatter Settlements," from the August 7, 1865, *Chicago Times*

THE CITY
Squatter Settlements.
Shanty Life in Chicago.
A Peculiar Institution of the Garden City.
The Patches of the Poor.
Where the Shanty Settlements are Located—Their Immense Population—Habits of the Squatters—The Fierceness of their Feuds. Kilgubbin and Kansas. Our Reporter's Invasion of these Classic Retreats. Scenes About the Shanties. Picturesque Glimpses of the Life in the Rough. &c. &c. &c.

Contrary to a prevalent opinion, Wells street does not contain all the wretchedness, poverty and vice of Chicago. Its crowded tenements and seething alleys of prostitution and crime are directly under the eye of the police, who never relax their relentless vigilance. There are other sources whence come frequent complaints, to annoy and puzzle the officers. These are the "patches" where the sons of the Emerald Isle have "squatted," built their seven-by-nine shanties, reared their offspring and bred their extensive droves of geese, hens, cows, dogs and cats. The progress of civilization, the rapid growth of the city, and the consequent increase in the value of property, do not seem to exert much influence upon these people. Wherever a block of land, or, perchance, a dreary sand hill along the lake, is in litigation, or of doubtful title, they find it out as if by instinct; up goes the shanty, which has perhaps been removed from some other locality upon the backs of the joint proprietors, Paddy and Biddy. This single land-mark having been erected, a village of shanties soon grow up, which can only be displaced by the whole police force united or by some action of the elements. A squatter clings to a piece of ground with bulldog tenacity. The unlucky owner of the property might as well attempt to depopulate half the city as to get them off his land. They are no more to be exterminated than are flies and mosquitoes. The shanty once erected, the pig sty built and the garden fenced in and planted, the squatter is as confident of his right of possession as if he held a deed of the land.

If a proprietor or land agent tells him to get off the premises, he laughs at the idea, and insists that he himself owns the place. If his residence is interfered with, he claims damages for trespass, and a long legal quarrel ensues, which obliges the real owner of the land to hunt up titles and surveys, until the thing has cost more money than the property is worth. Consequently a self possessed squatter remains undisturbed on his patch. If the first to find out the doubtful title of the land, the settlement that grows up around him is governed a good deal by what he says and does. He invites emigration to his patch, and an endless tide soon sets in. Woe be to the real estate agent, when such a hegira commences, and turns towards lands in his possession. His title is no longer worth the match to light it. As well might he attempt the conquest of the Brahmin empire, as to regain possession.

KILGUBBIN.

At the head of the list of the squatter villages of Chicago stands Kilgubbin, the largest shanty settlement within its limits. It has a varied history, having been the terror of constables, sherrifs and policemen in days that are past. It was, perhaps, the earliest settlement of the kind in Chicago, and at one time approached nearer to the squatter settlements of Gotham, than any other in the west. The advance of time and civilization has removed this classic locality several times. Its first site was on North Kinzie street, westward along the river *ad infinitum*. It numbered several years ago many thousand inhabitants, of all ages and habits, besides large droves of geese, goslings, pigs and rats. It was a safe retreat for criminals, policemen not venturing to invade its precincts, or even cross the border, without having a strong reserve force.

The Oldest inhabitants tell strange stories about murder and arson that hatched in this retreat, and children were frightened into submission by threats of being "sent to the Kilgubbin." The authorities finally got the better of them, and they gained more respect for the star of authority. Civilization pressed close in upon them, and the squatters emigrated slowly but surely westwards. Rude land owners and sheriffs rushed in upon the shanties, and demolished them; building mills, dwellings and manufactories on the old site of Kilgubbin. The squatters soon settled on other lands, and reared other villages.

The locality now known by that euphonious name is situated in the west division, northward of Chicago avenue, to the point where Carpenter street strikes the river. It extends north, south, east and west, in so many offshoots that it is difficult to define its exact limit. Where the shanties are there is Kilgubbin; and where a landlord has been bold enough to erect a building, Kilgubbin is not, until its shadow is passed. The present patch contains from forty to fifty acres of land, most of which is of doubtful title, in actual litigation, or owned by Eastern capitalists, who care little how it is occupied, so long as the growth of the city continues yearly to enhance its value.

A slight sketch of Kilgubbin society and of its private residences will convey an idea of squatter life generally. When the writer hereof visited that classic locality on Saturday morning, the weather was damp, and the unpaved streets of the settlement anything but "beautiful to the touch." The place was in possession of the women and children, the men having gone to their daily labor, in all quarters of the city. Here and there goose ponds were laid out in the streets, with great care as to effect. They were directly where a traveler wanted to step, and it was a long and muddy distance around them. Large flocks of goslings inhabit these stagnant pools; to kill or stone one of which would be instant death to the intruder. These geese cackle and hiss as you pass, as if no one but a resident had any business there. They seem to fear a land owner whenever a strange footstep is heard, an instinct early instilled into all the chattels of the squatter. They spread their wings and run off to the door of the nearest shanty. This brings the mistress out of doors, whose appearance may be briefly described:

The genuine squatter's wife is short and thick, with abundance of red hair and flesh. She is never without a broomstick in her hands, and never can be thrown off her guard. Her face is exceedingly red, and tells of "potations deep," and not the best quality. She is attired in a tattered dress, with sleeves rolled up. Barefoot is the latest style for the extremities, and she is in the fashion. She at once takes you for an eastern land owner, and is prepared to call together all the women of the patch, if she ascertains such to be the fact. If, however, you succeed in making her believe that you are a chance visitor, she becalms her passions, especially if a greenback is placed in her itching palm. Then she will show you through her shanty, and introduce you to her neighbors.

THE SHANTIES.

The shanties are generally divided into three apartments. In the first, which may be termed the parlor, are quartered the cow and pig. In the the second apartment, or the dining room, the goslings and geese, hens and chickens roost, secure from prowling marauders of policemen. Further on is the kitchen, considered the most magnificent room in the house, by the mistress thereof. If her cows, pigs, geese, goslings and hens are comfortably provided for, it does not matter any further. In this third apartment, separated from the others by a chinkless partition, are between ten and a dozen children, lying upon the floor in rows, in the most squalid rags and filth. A rickety bedstead serves for the proprietors of the establishment. This is the ultimatum of squatter desire. "Every thing under the same roof is secure," runs the proverb, which must have been well learned in Kilgubbin.

These shanties are almost boardless, or, at least, the majority of them. The elements find easy access, especially to the last mentioned apartment. They are sometimes inclosed by a low fence, and surrounded by a small patch of cabbages and potatoes, illy hoed and thriftless. How humanity can exist in such a place is a mystery.

KANSAS.

The region known as Kansas cannot be strictly called a squatter village, as most of the inhabitants pay a small rent for their shanties, or the land upon which they are built. It is situated on the west side of the river, between Desplaines and Halsted streets, in the neighborhood of Harrison. The land was formerly owned by an old Englishman, who is now dead. He has rented it to the squatters for a number of years. No citizen has been able to purchase it, although high prices have been offered for the land. The Morrison Brothers, who own property adjoining, have often tried to negotiate for it, but the landlord preferred to remain the proprietor of a squatter's village to selling his land for a fair price.

Like Kilgubbin, Kansas has been a place of terror to the authorities, but is not now what it was in former years. The inhabitants are quite orderly in their habit, and many of the men industrious laborers. Civilization has had a good effect upon the squatters, and they are disposed to profit by its approach. This tract contains in the neighborhood of eighteen or twenty acres of land, whereon are erected several hundred shanties, in close juxtaposition to each other. Like Kilgubbin, the manners and customs of its inhabitants are foreign in the extreme. But as a whole, the shanties are cleaner and more commodious. Some of them have creeping vines trained over the solitary window. The cows and pigs are in the rear. The front room is occupied as the residence. In one corner stands the bed, and at its foot the cupboard, whose shelves are filled with various colored crockery. In regard to actual comfort and neatness, Kansas is a squatter century ahead of Kilgubbin.

OTHER PATCHES.

Besides these two principal patches, there are scores of lesser ones scattered all over the city, from its center to the most remote boundaries. Wherever a block of land has remained unused for a short period, it has been appropriated, and now boasts of half a dozen shanties. Such a patch may be found on the west side, between Milwaukee avenue and Union street; another near North Rucker and Kinzie. A patch of some squatter pretensions is located on the north side, in the vicinity of Rees and Division streets, at the extreme limits of the city.

About one year ago, a village of several scores of shanties, situated on the South side, between State and Clark streets, near Twelfth street, was cleared out by the sheriff and a posse of police. The shanties were torn down over the heads of the obdurate squatters, and their pigs and cows driven off to the pound. Since this frightful "massacre," that locality has been comparatively free from geese and goslings, although in the vicinity of the quondam village, the soil still shows the traces of other fertilizers than lime and ashes. Here and there, all over the city, an occasional squatter can be found quietly enjoying the appropriated land of some unthinking capitalist. Some of these shanties have grown gray with years of unmolested existence; have stood there so long that the question of the title is no longer mooted—a very desirable way, it is submitted, of acquiring a residence.

SQUATTER FEUDS.

These squatters are a source of constant annoyance to the police, and to Justices of the Peace. Their appearance at the police court is by no means unfrequent. About a week ago, a case was narrated in this paper, where one squatter woman caused her neighbor to be arrested, because she allowed her geese to run on her patch, and scratch up her garden. The Judge could do nothing with the aggrieved parties. They bandied fierce words in court, and swore at each other in squatter jargon. They were finally both dismissed and told to go home. When crossing the threshold of the door, they got into a hand-to-hand row, and were called back and fined.

The females are extremely tenacious of their rights, and consequently, quarrel and fight among themselves, pull hair and disfigure eyes. In this respect a more turbulent race of people never existed. The women encourage their children to quarrel and fight, and teach them how it is done by actual combats with their neighbors. Every breeze blows dust into their eyes from somebody's patch with whom they are at loggerheads, and a fierce contest with shillelahs ensues. Thus these settlements are kept constantly in a state of turmoil and intestine war.

POPULATION.

The population of these patches cannot be correctly estimated. The census taker seldom attempts to enumerate the children and women he finds there. In some of the shanties reside five or six families, each being possessed of at least a dozen dirty ragamuffins. At the door of a small shanty in Kilgubbin, no less than thirty hatless and coatless brats were counted, besides whom there were probably "children in arms" inside the hut. It is estimated by persons well informed in regard to these squatter settlements that at least 15,000 people reside in them, within the city limits. This does not appear from a casual observation to be too great an estimate.

DESCRIPTIONS OF PROPERTY.

The presence of these intelligent squatters in any locality and the almost impossibility of getting rid of them short of a general extermination, has an injurious effect upon all kinds of property in their neighborhood. They prevent sales of lots, discourage owners from building houses which would tend to relieve the overcrowded parts of the city; and make every one who owns property there anxious to sell, and unwilling to make improvements. Men will not purchase property in their vicinity, any sooner than they would build a residence in the neighborhood of a permanent gipsey camp. Every attempt to displace them is followed by violence and crime. The whole squatter neighborhood regard the appearance of a land owner, or well dressed citizen in their midst as a *casus belli,* and sound their war cry at once. In a moment an army of infuriated women emerge from their cabins, armed with broomsticks and all manner of domestic implements of war. The venturesome person who dareth invade their haunts is driven away at the hight of his speed, barely escaping being ridden on a rail. The squatter therefore becomes quite as secure in his shanty as the proprietor of a mansion on Michigan avenue, and feels his importance quite as much.

"With a pipe in his mouth sat Paddy so free,
No king in his palace is prouder than he."

SQUATTER ANNOYANCES.

Persons so unfortunate as to reside in the vicinity of one of these settlements, suffer the greatest annoyance from the flocks of geese and hens, sows and pigs, that constantly trespass upon their premises. Leaving the troops of ragged, dirty, yelling ragamuffins out of sight, these animals fill the neighboring streets and take possession of the sidewalks with the utmost *nonchalance*. They rub against gates and force them open. Attempt to drive a squatter's cow out of your yard and straightway there appears a score of infuriated urchins, set on by the women, who pounce upon you and rescue the animal from chastisement. The shrubbery of private grounds is thus browsed upon and the yards defaced. Enter a complaint at the police station, and instantly upon the receipt of the news at the settlement, a squad of old harridans will pounce upon your premises and destroy everything within their reach. It is no wonder, in view of these inevitable consequences, that property in the neighborhood of squatter villages depriciates in value.

WILL THEY FINALLY BE DISPERSED?

The history of Kilgubbin shows that in due process of time these squatter settlements will be entirely displaced. The yearly growth of the city encroaches upon them and so their localities are constantly changing.

A combined movement on the part of property holders might dispossess them, but such an organized movement is difficult and almost impracticable. The matter lies mostly in the hands of land owners. When they sell their property they will be obliged to bring to bear a large force of police, else they can never give possession of it. Seven cases were recently entered in the Supreme Court in one day against these parties, by land holders, who claim the land upon which they are living. The squatters were notified at the time. The decision in these cases may be taken as a precedent in the matter of dispossessing them finally.

References

Andreas, A. T. History of Chicago. Vol. 2. New York: Arno Reprint, 1975.

Bailey's Chicago City Directory for the year 1865–66. Chicago: John C. W. Bailey, Publisher, 1865.

Bailey's Chicago City Directory for the Year 1866–67. Chicago: John C. W. Bailey, 1866.

Biographical Directory of the American Congress, 1774–1971. Washington, D. C.: U.S. Government Printing Office, 1971.

Blanchard, R. *Blanchard's Guide to Chicago.* Chicago: R. Blanchard, 1866.

Bush, Conrad. Biographical information on Charles T. Phelan. Personal communication, Jan. 25, 2000.

———. "Roster of the 24th Independent Battery New York Light Artillery, formerly Company B, Rocket Battalion." <http://home.att.net/~cwppds/24nyroster.htm> December 20, 2001. Roster posted by Conrad Bush, 24th NY Independant Battery Historian for the Civil War Plymouth Pilgrims Descendants Society.

Check List of Chicago Ante-Fire Imprints, 1851–1871. Chicago: The Historical Records Survey, 1938.

Chicago Republican, 1865–66.

Chicago Times, 1865.

Chicago Tribune, 1865–66.

Currey, J. Seymour. *Chicago: Its History and Its Builders.* Chicago: S. J. Clarke Publishing Co, 1912.

Drury, John. "Historic Chicago Sites: Camp Fry." Undated article in the library of the Chicago Historical Society.

Edwards' Annual Directory to . . . Chicago for 1866. Chicago: Edwards, Greenough & Deved, 1866.

Frank Leslie's Illustrated Newspaper (New York), Nov. 3, 1866.

Gilbert, Paul, and Charles Lee Bryson. *Chicago and Its Makers.* Chicago: F. Mendelsohn, Publishers, 1929.

Goodrich, DeWitt. *An Illustrated History of the State of Indiana.* Indianapolis: R. S. Peale and Company, 1875.

Halpin's Seventh Annual Chicago City Directory 1864–5. Comp. T. M. Halpin. Chicago: T. M. Halpin, 1864. Printed by the Religio-Philosophical Publishing Association.

Halpin's Eighth Annual Chicago City Directory 1865–6. Comp. T. M. Halpin. Chicago: T. M. Halpin, 1865. Printed by the Religio-Philosophical Publishing Association.

Hewett, Janet B., ed. *The Roster of Union Soldiers, 1861–1865: New York.* Wilmington, N.C.: Broadfoot Publishing Company, 1998.

References Johnson, Allen, and Dumas Malone, eds. *Dictionary of American Biography*. New York: Charles Scribner's Son, 1927–36.

Macon County Chamber of Commerce. "Andersonville Prisoner Lookup." A database of the names of over 32,000 prisoners. <http://www.maconcountyga.org/> December 20, 2001.

Merrill, Julian W. *Records of the 24th Independent Battery, N.Y. Light Artillery, U.S.V.* Published for the Ladies' Cemetery Association of Perry, N.Y, 1870.

National Union Catalogue, Pre-1956 Imprints. London & Chicago: Mansell and American Library Association, 1968–80.

Odell, George C. D. *Annals of the New York Stage*. Vol. 7 (1857–65). New York: Columbia University Press, 1931.

Oxford Companion to American Theatre. New York: Oxford University Press, 1992.

Pierce, Bessie Louise. *A History of Chicago*. Vol. 2. New York: Knopf, 1940.

Random House Historical Dictionary of American Slang. Vol. 2. New York: Random House, 1997.

Report of the Condition of the Soldier's Home in Chicago for the Year Ending June 25th, 1880. Chicago: n.p., n.d.

Sheahan, James W. *Chicago Illustrated*. Chicago: Jevne and Almini, 1866–67.

Sinkevitch, Alice, ed. *AIA Guide to Chicago*. New York: Harcourt Brace & Company, 1993.

Soldiers' Home Second Anniversay Reports of Officers. Chicago: Np, 1865.

Spencer, Ambrose. *A Narrative of Andersonville*. New York: Harper & Brothers, Publishers, 1866.

Trebbel, John. *An American Dynasty*. New York: Doubleday, 1947.

Walsh, Justin E. *To Print the News and Raise Hell! A Biography of Wilbur F. Storey*. Chapel Hill: University of North Carolina Press, 1968.

Williams, Kenny J. *Prairie Voices: A Literary History of Chicago from the Frontier to 1893*. Nashville, Tenn.: Townsend Press, 1980.

Wilt, Napier. *Drama Performance Index* [Chicago]. Napier Wilt Papers. The University of Chicago Libraries, Special Collections.

Index

Page numbers in italics refer to illustrations.

Index

Robert Williams is the assistant design manager of the University of Chicago Press and a longtime student of the history of printing and calligraphy. He has published articles and contributed to several encyclopedias on the history of calligraphy, and his own calligraphic work is in both public and private collections in the United States and Europe.